Complicities

Complicities:
The People's Republic of China in Global Capitalism

Arif Dirlik

PRICKLY PARADIGM PRESS
CHICAGO

© 2017 Arif Dirlik.
All rights reserved.

Prickly Paradigm Press, LLC
5629 South University Avenue
Chicago, IL 60637

www.prickly-paradigm.com

ISBN: 9780996635530
LCCN: 2017934556

Printed in the United States of America on acid-free paper.

Contents

I. Introduction.. 1

II. The Idea of a "Chinese Model":
A Critical Discussion... 13

III. Social Justice, Democracy and the Politics of
Development: The People's Republic of China
in Global Perspective.. 45

IV. Forget Tiananmen, You Don't Want to Hurt
the Chinese People's Feelings—and Miss Out on
the Business of the New 'New China'!............................. 79

V. Mme. Xu's Excellent Adventure, or,
What the PRC Wants.. 109

VI. The Rise of China—
and the End of the World as We Know It.................... 127

Dedicated with deep respect and admiration to all those from the PRC to Turkey—and elsewhere—who at great personal risk uphold citizens' and human rights against oppressive power.

I
Introduction

This collection of essays on politics and development in the People's Republic of China (PRC) share two premises that I hope will be apparent to the reader: (a) the integration of the PRC into global capitalism over the last two decades requires criticism directed at it also to attend to the structure of the system of which it is a part, and, (b) given the economic, social political, and cultural entanglements of global capitalism, criticism must account for outsiders' complicities materially and ideologically in the PRC's failures as well as successes. There is more at stake in a critical understanding of the PRC than the fate of the PRC itself. For the same reason, criticism that ignores the relationships that in their very fluidity dynamize global politics and culture, and fails to reflect on the self in criticism of the other, more often than not simply falls back upon received ideological or cultural shibboleths, if it does not slide into vacuous self-righteousness.

PRC's development over the last three decades has been greeted with enthusiasm, albeit mixed with a good dose of anxiety. Most often noted among its achievements are accumulation of wealth on a sufficient scale to reconfigure the global distribution of wealth and poverty, large-scale poverty reduction as measured by global institutions such as the World Bank, seemingly overnight urbanization of a paradigmatic agrarian society, and creation of a "middle class" large and hungry enough to raise global consumption to unprecedented levels. Less conspicuous but no less significant is the impact of the PRC's "rise" on societies of the Global South not only as a source of investment and affordable commodities but as a rival to advanced capitalist societies that has opened up new spaces for political maneuver.

Other achievements evoke greater ambivalence, among them the PRC's rise to global power status that challenges the order (or disorder, depending on perspective) secured by US hegemony, and what sometimes sounds like bragging rights to be #1 in everything from global trade and voracious consumption of raw materials to environmental destruction at home and, increasingly, abroad. It has drawn ongoing criticism for its abuse of human rights, perversion of its own laws in the suppression of citizens' rights and freedoms, creation of one of the most unequal societies in the contemporary world out of one of the most equal only three decades ago, dispossession and exploitation of the agrarian population, forced dislocation of millions to make room for megaprojects that would be the envy of any "oriental despotism," colonial occupation of minority lands most egregiously in Tibet and Xinjiang, imperious belligerence toward Taiwan and Hong Kong, irredentist claims based on spurious historical evidence to justify expansion of its boundaries, and, most consequentially from a global perspective, a reckless developmentalism driven by a "great leap" mentality and oiled by corruption. The popular quasi-religious zeal inflamed by the regime that pushed the revolutionary movement to self-destructive extremes under Mao Zedong, shorn of all revolutionary aspirations, serves under his successors the pursuit of wealth and power by any means necessary, with the same urgency regardless of consequences. In the words of the dissident writer, Yu Hua, "within China's success story one can see both revolutionary movements reminiscent of the Great Leap Forward and revolutionary violence that recalls the Cultural Revolution."

These criticisms may have tarnished the PRC's image to some extent, at least among some constituencies. They have done little so far to diminish the deference it commands or to provoke serious international repercussions against its abuse of human rights at home or greedy aggressive behavior abroad. Its great power status gives it immunity from the reprisals visited upon less powerful states for similar transgressions, but does not explain the continued adulation it enjoys. Corporate capital, which has repeatedly demonstrated its contempt for human rights and social justice, is heavily invested in the PRC as a source—so far—of cheap labor and wealthy customers. Global institutions from the IMF and World Bank to the United Nations Development Program routinely bemoan the social and environmental toll the PRC's "rise" has taken, and just as routinely turn around to celebrate its success in "poverty reduction"(as they define it), and the creation of a "middle class"—more accurately a "consuming class" as some would call it—that has opened up new horizons of consumption—as if the celebrated consumption had nothing to do with the bemoaned destruction that has brought the ecological horizon of human existence into visible range. The PRC has emerged regardless as a source of inspiration to those desirous of emulating its "rise" in global capitalism, or joining the bandwagon it seeks to cobble together to challenge the existing global order of which it has been the beneficiary, but still short of achieving the hegemony it dreams of. There are leftists, opposed to capitalism and desperate to salvage what they can of a lost socialism, who manage to take seriously the "socialism" in the so-called "socialism with Chinese characteristics," willing to overlook that the "characteristics" consist most conspicuously of Party dictatorship, a new class rule structured by an alliance between political and economic power, cultivation of a chauvinistic nationalism among the population, and suppression of any notion of socialism or Marxism other than what is dictated by sanctimonious slogans of successive leaders that pass for "theoretical" contributions. Socialism also suffers caricaturization at the hands of right-wing detractors of the PRC unable or unwilling to distinguish between communism and a party dictatorship deeply entangled in capitalism, as well as unlikely defenders among the more hare-brained apologists for the so-called Confucius Institutes who seek to discredit critics by misplaced charges of "anti-communism" and "McCarthyism."

There has been a veritable cult of "China" for the last three decades which, given how much more we know about the country, easily surpasses the *Chinoiserie* of the 17th and 18th centuries. The Confucius Institutes on US campuses (and around the world) may be the most eloquent testimonial to this cult. Established through "confidential" negotiations between the PRC's Hanban (literally, Han language classrooms) and unscrupulous university administrators, the institutes transgress against even moderate notions of "conflict of interest" between donor demands and educational autonomy. That the donor in this case is a propaganda organ of a foreign state propaganda apparatus tasked with promoting "soft power" adds an unprecedented dimension to the conflict of interest. Widespread criticism from authoritative educational bodies goes largely unheeded even if it possibly has played some part in embarrassing several prestigious institutions to cut their ties to the Hanban over the past year or so. It has not stopped a US educational leader from singing the praises of the Hanban in the servile cultic language that PRC Red Guards and their foreign mimics of a previous generation reserved for the sainted Chairman Mao. At a meeting honoring Xu Lin, the notorious head of Hanban, the President of the US College Board David Coleman reportedly declaimed, "Hanban is just like the sun. It lights the path to develop Chinese teaching in the U.S…The College Board is the moon. I am so honored to reflect the light that we've gotten from Hanban."

The cult blends neoliberal celebrations of "China's rise" with a long-standing fascination with Chinese exceptionalism. Circuits of image-making at work for half a millennium account in part for the deference extended to the PRC's leadership that on occasion is reminiscent of the prostrations expected of tributary envoys by their imperial predecessors. In the end, however, it is the expectation of financial largesse and the promise of untold profits to be made that plays the most important and conspicuous part in securing compliance with PRC wishes. Unlike during the Cold

War, the claims PRC leaders make on the existing world order are justified not by the offer of an alternative to capitalism or even an alternative ideology, but the example of efficient capitalist development under an authoritarian state, laced with memories of the imperial tribute system. What they have to offer by way of persuasion is simply—and quite openly—"money."

In his shocking account of environmental and social devastation in Tibet, the Canadian writer Michael Buckley suggests that Party leaders suffer from a "tunnel vision" in their faith that the answer to problems created by development is more development. That is indeed the case, reaffirmed by successive leaders. Unfortunately, however, the faith is not just a PRC thing but is imbedded in the vision that drives global capitalism. From environmental destruction to social inequality, the problems that plague the PRC's development are global problems across divides of developed and developing nations. Possibly the most important aspect of the PRC's development that for obvious reasons rarely finds its way into even critical discussions has been to demonstrate the unsustainability of a globalized capitalism. The very same development that is responsible for the improved welfare of the PRC population is the cause of the damage it has inflicted on the environment, anxiety about resources that drives both further destruction and colonial activity, and the social, political and intellectual contradictions that invite ongoing political oppression and ideological policing. These signs of "maldevelopment" may not be attributed merely to the stresses and contradictions created by the incompatibility between a capitalist economy and Bolshevik politics (or legacies that lie in more distant pasts). One important reason PRC leaders have difficulty in dealing with the problems the country faces is that the problems are the other side of the coin to their successes, and it seems nearly impossible to overcome them without abandoning the development that for better *and* worse has brought them to where they are. It may be too late to backtrack now in face of the new constituencies development has created. PRC leaders have made quite clear their commitment to protect the new capitalist class development has created. At the same time, it is quite telling that any sign of efforts to slow down development to attend to the problems it has created is greeted by howls of protest among the constituencies of global capital. The PRC has become the engine of global capitalism, but only at the cost of becoming its captive.

One can hardly dispute PRC scholars and political commentators who point out that US and European advanced capitalist societies did far more ecological damage in the course of their development (and still do), engaged in unspeakable acts of colonial oppression and plunder (and still do), enslaved millions of Africans and exterminated countless indigenous people physically and culturally, and, of course, produced tyrannical regimes against which the Party dictatorship in the PRC seems like garden–variety benevolent despotism. These objections carry considerable historical and moral weight. They ignore, however, that the point is to learn from the past in order not to repeat the mistakes and crimes of others, not to use their example to justify similar mistakes and crimes at the present. The argument that further development will alleviate some of the worst problems such as environmental destruction and social inequality is meaningless within the context of an earth reaching the limits of its ability to sustain life, and against the evidence of severe inequality in advanced capitalist societies.

More pertinent in an immediate sense is indisputable evidence that the same advanced capitalist societies have been complicit in the social and environmental consequences of the PRC's development both as direct participants in production and indirect beneficiaries in consumption. Within the context of global capitalism, the PRC is distinguished most importantly by its successful navigation (or, from a less charitable perspective, manipulation) of the rules of the game, backed by a coherent political organization and a population practiced in social and political engagement, both of them the legacies of decades of revolutionary mobilization. The "great leap" mentality that had grave consequences for the PRC population under Mao Zedong is equally visible in contemporary policies—with the difference that whereas for Mao it was a test of revolutionary zeal, the post-revolutionary leadership has deployed it in the service of self-aggrandizement, predatory economic and social relationships, and the pursuit of national economic and political power. The transition from revolutionary austerity to the consumptive freedoms of a market economy, however incomplete, has no doubt been quite exhilarating. But that is no reason to overlook the new forms of predation that have appeared in the course of the transition that may be even more destructive in the long run not just for the PRC but the whole world. Mao's policies are roundly condemned in our day—for some good reasons but also as part of a general condemnation of revolutions. His successors enjoy immunity from criticism, if they are not held in awe for their achievements which find ready acceptance as they emulate with ruthless determination patterns of production and consumption established by advanced capitalist societies, especially the US. Interestingly, whereas Mao's China inspired a previous generation of radicals for its promise of an alternative to the destructive consumerism of advanced capitalist societies, post-revolutionary PRC draws its admirers most prominently from those who view it as a bottomless reservoir of consumers to nourish a faltering capitalism in perpetual crisis.

Politically, too, it is misleading to isolate the PRC's problems from those of its global context. PRC leaders' refusal to grant political participation in any form—even with "Chinese characteristics"—to their citizens does not seem out of the ordinary when democracy is under threat everywhere, including democratic societies where popular rights are undermined by a combination of social inequality and ever more intrusive policing of increasingly incoherent populations. The alliance between economic and political power to the detriment of populations at large is not limited to the PRC, or authoritarian societies alone. It is no wonder that Party ideologues perceive in the contemporary global situation an opportunity for exporting the so-called "China model," which is little more than an authoritarian version of capitalism freed from such encumbrances as human rights and democratic politics.

They have good reason for their confidence. Their campaigns against "contamination" by "Western values" find alibi abroad not only among those who have little concern for those values except as instruments of policy, but in educational institutions supposedly founded upon those very values. The PRC has suffered no repercussions of significance for its novel "solution" to the problem of human rights in mid-2015: jailing human rights lawyers on trumped-up charges! The response of "Western" institutions to the suppression of dissent and human rights is to welcome the Confucius Institutes intended to spread "Chinese" values. More recently, US hedge-fund manager Stephen Schwarzman has initiated the China-equivalent of the Rhodes scholarship at Tsinghua University in Beijing to cultivate a Sino-American elite. Its governing board includes such luminaries as Henry Kissinger and Tony Blair, favorites of the PRC leadership and other like-minded despotic regimes who retain lucrative influence in global affairs despite the stigma of war crimes that has dogged them for their deeds while in office. Criticism of PRC leadership for their determination to keep at arm's length values of human rights and democracy is bound to fall on deaf ears so long as they are routinely compromised in their original homelands.

I owe a debt of gratitude to a number of colleagues and friends who read and commented on one or another of these essays when they were initially published, or who in discussions have contributed to my understanding of the issues I take up. These issues present profound historical, political and ethical uncertainties. Their encouragement was much appreciated. I would like to name, in particular, David Bartel, Veysel Batmaz, Paul Bove, Cao Tianyu, Yinha Chan, Stephen Chu, Ya-Chung Chuang, Christopher Connery, Lin Chun, Liu Dong, Yige Dong, Michael Dutton, Harry Harootunian, Ruth Hung, Dongyoun Hwang, Nick Knight, John Lagerwey, Victor Mair, Tak-wing Ngo, Roxann Prazniak, Stuart Souther, Timothy Summers, Mette Thunoe, QS Tong, Sebastian Veg, Wang Guo, Wang Mingming, Rob Wilson, Shaobo Xie, Emile Kok-KhengYeoh, and Yu Keping. I also would like to acknowledge the input of participants in conferences on the "China Model" organized by the Central Compilation and Translation Bureau (Beijing) and the

Marxism Academy of the Chinese Academy of Social Sciences. I am grateful for their graciousness to the audiences at the Vancouver Institute, the Humanities Center at the University of Pittsburgh, and the "Critical Dialogues About China" seminar at Hong Kong University where the concluding essay was presented as lectures.

The articles included in this volume were first published in *China Information* ("China Model") and *International Journal of China Studies* ("Social Justice" and "June 4"). I thank the editors, Tak-wing Ngo and Emile Yeh respectively, for their permission to reprint them here. I am grateful to Marshall Sahlins for his encouragement to compile these essays for publication in the Prickly Paradigm series, which is where I think they belong. I have revised the essays slightly from the originals to eliminate redundancies. I ask the reader's indulgence for some of the overlap that remains which is intentional, to preserve the integrity of the individual essays. I have tried throughout to avoid the use of the terms China and Chinese in favor of the official name of the country, the People's Republic of China, and *huaren*, which refers to "Chinese" in general without the implication of citizenship in any one country.

II
The Idea of a "Chinese Model": A Critical Discussion

I would like to take up in this discussion some questions thrown up by the idea of a "Chinese model." As far as I am aware the idea of a model originated from foreigners of various stripes anxious to discover a categorical encapsulation of the PRC's development, to be embraced subsequently by PRC leaders and writers anxious to establish a developmental identity of their own. The term itself has appeared with increasing frequency over the last decade among both PRC scholars and foreign observers. Against the continued economic difficulties faced by the US, Europe and Japan, the seeming success of the PRC in weathering the world recession since 2008 has enhanced the significance of the "model," giving it all the trappings of official discourse.

There is a suggestion in this official discourse, and among those who serve as its voices, of a model that is not only superior to the reigning neo-liberal orthodoxy, promoted most enthusiastically by the United States and United Kingdom, but also, given the remarkably rapid development of the PRC over the last three decades, to the development path pioneered by Euro/American societies since the origins of capitalist modernization in the eighteenth century. Yet, what this model consists of, and how it may be translated into different social and political contexts, remains quite vague. It is not very helpful, as such self-serving claims suggest, that as the idea has acquired prominence, it has become the subject of political manipulation by both opponents and proponents of the Communist regime at home and abroad, as well as those who benefit from the PRC's development, or hope to do so, and those who suffer the consequences of policies associated with the idea.

There are methodological problems as well. The laundry list approach that characterizes most discussions simply draws on a variety of policies pursued by the regime to render what may be contingent responses into a "model," with its suggestion of conscious design, so that even "pragmatism," which resists such categorization, is rendered into the terms of the discourse. At the other extreme are obscurantist references to exceptional Chinese characteristics that by definition rule out the possibility of the PRC's development serving as a model of any kind. Only occasionally is there any kind of effort to distill from a wide array of shifting practical policies an account of the structural premises coherent enough to justify the use of the term, model. Even then, there is a conspicuous absence of attention to the historical circumstances that may be crucial to understanding the ideological and practical forces that have guided the development of PRC society.

These considerations guide the discussion below. Three questions are of particular interest in this discussion. First, what significance do we attribute to the idea of a "model" in the contemporary world, especially with respect to the deployment of the idea of model within a PRC political discourse. Secondly, what might be the features of a so-called "Chinese model?" And, finally, in what sense might this "model" be appealing to others, especially over the neo-liberal model of a market economy theoretically unfettered by social and political intervention but also in its own right, as a socialist path of development? I will conclude with brief commentaries on the relevance of "Chinese Marxism" to the official conceptualization the PRC's development of the model and its implications as a global idea.

Global Modernity and the Chinese Model

The idea of a "Chinese model" may refer to a model of development that is peculiar to the PRC, appropriate to the particular circumstances of PRC society. Or it may be understood in universalistic terms, as a model open to emulation by others, in which case its relevance transcends the boundaries of PRC society.

The distinction is an important one, even if it is ignored in most references to the "Chinese model." If the model is a product of the particular circumstances of PRC society, the implication is that it may not be emulated by others, or may be emulated only with adjustment to different circumstances and needs. This is indeed the way the Chinese experience as an example for others has been understood in Chinese political discourse going back to the 1940s. Within Marxism and the history of socialist revolutions, the Chinese Revolution was the first (if not the only) one to insist on the necessity of articulating the universalist discourse of theory to concrete local circumstances, as is clearly implied by principles encapsulated in such phrases as "Making Marxism Chinese" (*Makesi zhuyide Zhongguohua*), "Chinese style socialism" (*Zhongguo shide shehui zhuyi*), or, most recently, "Socialism with Chinese characteristics" (*you Zhongguo tesede shehui zhuyi*). The strategy of revolution or development expressed by these phrases, themselves alternative Chinese "models," distinguished the Chinese path not only from capitalist societies but also from other socialisms, most importantly that of the Soviet Union while it existed. There has been a sense all along that the experience of the Chinese Revolution was relevant to all societies placed similarly to China in global politics, so-called "semi-feudal and semi-colonial" societies, which in an earlier day made China a part of both the second and the third worlds. But throughout, the Chinese experience provided not a path to be followed but an example of articulating the universal to the particular, or translating the global to the local, which called upon others to find *their* own paths by following a similar procedure. This idea of a revolutionary practice that necessarily integrated universal principles with concrete local circumstances distinguished the path of revolution not only from one national context to another but also applied to different localities within the same nation. The "vernacularization" of Marxism has been one of the significant contributions of the Chinese Revolution to Marxist theory. Despite significant transformations over the years, it has characterized Chinese Marxism throughout, in Maoist as well as post-Maoist Marxism. This attitude toward the Chinese Revolution has been extended in Chinese Marxism to revolutions and development elsewhere.

This distinction between a universal model and practices informed by universal principles but ultimately derivative of local circumstances is more important than ever under the regime of global modernity, characterized by an insistence on national or local particularity within the context of a globalized capitalism. We have witnessed over the last two decades a proliferation of calls for "alternative modernities" even as the globalization of capitalism has restricted if not abolished spaces within which to imagine and construct such alternatives. One important consequence has been a simultaneous proliferation of "models." There are no longer just two or three models as in the days of the Cold War, but an increasing number of them. We encounter daily references to the "Iranian model," the

"Turkish model," the "Indonesian model," the "Indian model," and many others, as changing circumstances around the world call attention to one or another example of development deemed relevant by various constituencies.

It is possible that "the Chinese model" was responsible at least in part for the stress on particular modernities, and it continues to inspire faith in the possibility of alternatives. It is more difficult to judge its significance. It may be suggested that there were always significant differences between societies, and that no two capitalisms or socialisms are entirely alike. The difference between the present and the past may lie not in the novelty of difference but in a heightened consciousness of and will to difference. The Cold War no doubt disguised the many differences of the day by subordinating them to a binary or tripartite division of the world. So did the hegemonic discourse of modernization, capitalist or socialist, with its own binarisms of progressive and traditional, or advanced and backward. The globalization of modernity ironically has brought to the surface a consciousness of difference that also has set off a search for different paths of development, especially in those societies empowered by success in the global economy. And there seems to be no shortage of models for development, even if they don't command equal degrees of attention. Still, if there is a Chinese model, it is one of many.

In light of these considerations, would it make more sense to speak of a "Chinese paradigm" (*moshi* or *fanshi*) rather than a Chinese model (*mofan, moshi*), which would shift attention from an example to be emulated to an example that provides not only inspiration but also procedural principles, central to which is attentiveness to the possibilities and limitations of concrete local circumstances as well as location in the world? This is not only consistent with the legacies of the Chinese Revolution and socialist thinking, but respond more closely to the ideological tendencies of global modernity. It would also avoid the ambiguities of the idea of a "Chinese model," with its implications of an establish pattern, that hardly does justice to what may be but a work in progress, a subject itself of ongoing experimentation.

Is There a Chinese Model?

The question I would like to raise here is whether the idea of a "Chinese model" is based on a substantial set of norms and practices, or derives its meaning primarily from its contrasts with liberalism or neo-liberalism, much as the similar idea of a "Beijing consensus" (*Beijing gongshi*, coined by a Goldman Sachs employee for a presentation sponsored by Tony Blair) acquired a hearing some years back for its supposed contrasts to the "Washington consensus?" If that is indeed the case, secondly, do we need a further specification of its goals, and whether or not those goals pertain simply to issues of economic development, or include social and political goals as well. After all, simply being different from neo-liberalism does not tell us much about whether or not the "model" points toward socialism, or other, possibly more conservative goals as a version of authoritarian developmentalism, associated in the late 1980s with so-called "new authoritarianism" (*xin quanwei zhuyi*).

If it is possible to speak of a Chinese model, it is indeed closest to this latter idea, which bears a close kinship to a socialism that has been stripped of its more radical aspirations to create a just and egalitarian society free of the exploitative relations characteristic of earlier modes of production, including capitalism. Traceable to the inspiration of Samuel P. Huntington's 1969 publication, *Political Order in Changing Societies*, "new authoritarianism" was associated early on with the developmental paths followed most effectively by a number of Eastern Asian societies, namely, Japan, South Korea, Taiwan, Singapore and Hong Kong under British colonial rule. Following WW II, especially from the 1960s, these regimes achieved rapid development under a combination of political authoritarianism (or dictatorship) and sub-contractual economic development, beginning with the creation of export zones, that would serve as the pioneering moments in the emergence of "a new international division of labor," neo-liberal assaults on national economic boundaries and, ultimately, what has come to be known as globalization. In the traditionalism which underwrote their authoritarianism, these regimes also pointed to the cultural resurgences that would come with globalization, challenging the Eurocentric assumptions of an earlier modernization discourse. The result was also the stripping down of modernity to its technologies, which served different social, political and cultural trajectories, with success dependent on historical circumstances, with cultural legacies allegedly playing a crucial role. It was the developmental success of Eastern Asian societies that empowered the Confucian revival of the 1980s that since then has served as an explanation of their success.

The so-called "Chinese model" may be considered one more variant of authoritarian development that in its origins owed much to these societies both for inspiration and for direct involvement in triggering its take-off. Contemporary discussions not only in the PRC but also among many foreign commentators display a remarkable "forgetfulness" concerning the part that the Japanese, South Korean, Taiwanese, but especially the Singaporean "models" played in inspiring policy in the initial phase of "reform and opening" (*gaige kaifang*) in the 1980s and through the 1990s. But their significance goes beyond the inspiration they provided. The flourishing economies of Eastern Asia provided a context for the development of the PRC in which they played a strategically crucial part. It may be no exaggeration to say that investments and technological input from these societies, as well as from Overseas Chinese in Southeast Asia were responsible for bringing the PRC economy to its take-off stage. This context is also one of the particularities of the PRC's development that call into question its emulation by others.

There are two important historical differences, nevertheless, that distinguish the PRC's development from that of these neighboring neo-authoritarian regimes that also receive little attention these days, especially among outside commentators. The PRC when it launched its modernization program after 1978 was the product of one of the most important revolutions of the century, heralding the political and economic reemergence of the colonial, "semi-colonial and semi-feudal" worlds through movements for national liberation. In this case, it was a national liberation movement imbued with socialist goals. The liberation of the nation was to be grounded in a social and cultural revolution. It may be noted that other societies of the region also went through social transformations of one kind or another as a condition of development, from the reconstitution of Japanese society after WWII to land reform in Taiwan to anti-colonial movements in Singapore, Korea, and Hong Kong. Unlike in these societies where the transformations created new social hierarchies consistent with development within the capitalist system, the Chinese Revolution sought a social and cultural transformation toward the creation of a socialist society that stressed egalitarianism, giving a voice to the people, and the creation of a new culture consistent with these goals. The legacy of egalitarianism has been significant not only in shaping the trajectory of Chinese development but also in cushioning new inequalities generated by capitalist development, most importantly in the countryside.

Another very significant difference was also the goal and a byproduct of the revolution: autonomous and self-reliant development. Transformations in the rest of the societies of the region were accomplished under the aegis of imperial powers, most importantly after WWII the US. In the case of the PRC, avoiding foreign domination of the economy (capitalist or socialist) was a fundamental premise and goal of the revolution. Self-reliance, moreover, was equally important for regional as for national development. In the reform period, the importance of the legacies of local self-reliance has been demonstrated most effectively in the part played by local cadres in development projects (also the source, conversely, of corrupt practices that are a major source of popular disaffection—and political headache for the central authorities). Self-reliance also made possible the high rate of savings that enabled the state to extract the maximum amount of surplus from the countryside to finance development.

What is remarkable about discussions of the "Chinese model" idea is the obliviousness to this historical trajectory that makes China unique and, therefore, difficult if not impossible to emulate. China as we know it today is a product of this revolution, which unfortunately is often beclouded by the claims to continuity with a so-called 5000 years of tradition of a resurgent traditionalism that covers over the revolution (which is described in the new Museum of History in Beijing as "period of rejuvenation"). The fervent nationalism that has drawn much scholarly attention since the 1990s was the product of ideological activity that accompanied the renunciation of revolution in the early 1980s. The revolutionary nationalism of an earlier period that linked the struggle against imperialism with a social revolution at home has been replaced by a de-revolutionized nationalism which places at the fore the patriotic struggles of all Chinese, which has come to encompass all Chinese globally. Combined with assertions of timeless Chinese culture, it lends a strong racial tinge to the understanding of "Chineseness." It is a far cry, at any rate, from the more complicated nationalism of an earlier period driven by a more strictly social and political understanding of the nation. Forgotten in the process is the contribution to the reforms of the experience and organizational legacies of the revolution.

More often than not, that same revolution has been rendered into a "negative example" for its failures, which were real but only part of the story. Deploying the revolution as a foil against which to claim legitimacy for the present has covered over its legacies to the present, both positive and negative. Thus it is hardly mentioned that during the revolutionary years before 1978 the economy developed rapidly, registering annual growth rates that match the much-touted rates of the post-1978 period. While occasions of ill-considered enthusiasm had disastrous consequences for the people, and self-reliant development required extraction of excessive amounts of surplus from the people, especially in rural areas, there was nevertheless ongoing improvement in people's lives from education and health care to increases in life expectancy. The social transformation that the revolution sought may have been less than perfect, but it came with an organizational transformation that unified and integrated the country, laying the infrastructure that would serve well after 1978. These changes also created a new culture of politics and work, the significance of which for later development is yet to be analyzed. On the other hand, while the organizational achievements of the revolution lay the foundation for subsequent development, they also stood in the way of further changes necessitated by development in a new direction. The greatest achievement of the Reform period has been the removal of the obstacles while making use of these earlier achievements.

There is also a tendency to downplay the national liberation aspects of the struggle, more its economic and cultural than its political aspects. China's economic "globalization" is now extended back over time, erasing the problematic relationship with the outside world that marked the last two centuries. Culture has been nationalized, but now it is continuity with the past that is stressed rather than the dialectical discontinuity called for by the revolution. Political colonialism is remembered in the stress on past "national humiliation," but it is accompanied also by its erasure, as for instance in the literature on the Shanghai Expo celebrating its continuity with past world expositions while by-passing the racial discrimination and humiliations China had suffered in early twentieth century fairs.

The point here is not that these things should be remembered to foster continued suspicion and hostility, but because they are important to assessing the meaning of "the Chinese model" beyond its reductionist economistic understanding. Divorced from the legacies of the revolution, the "Chinese model" becomes one more version of authoritarian development, seeking ideological and cultural compliance with the demands of development as a participant in the global capitalist economy, without any concerns beyond success in this economy. This is how it is widely perceived in the PRC, and by admirers of its development abroad. To cite one recent convert from neo-liberalism to the "Chinese model," Francis Fukuyama:

> The most important strength of the Chinese political system is its ability to make large, complex decisions quickly, and to make them relatively well, at least in economic policy. This is most evident in the area of infrastructure, where China has put into place airports, dams, high-speed rail, water and electricity systems to feed its growing industrial base. Contrast this with [democratic] India, where every new investment is subject to blockage by trade unions, lobby groups, peasant associations and courts...Nonetheless, the quality of Chinese government is higher than in Russia, Iran, or the other authoritarian regimes with which it is often lumped—precisely because Chinese rulers feel some degree of accountability towards their population. That accountability is not, of course, procedural; the authority of the Chinese Communist party is limited neither by a rule of law nor by democratic elections. But while its leaders limit public criticism, they do try to stay on top of popular discontents, and shift policy in response.

Fukuyama's observations may be exemplary of most discussions of the "China model." What makes it work is its deficit of democracy. Authoritarianism makes possible the rapid and efficient mobilization of resources not possible in a democratic society, exemplified by India, another so-called "developing economy." The Party-state may be repressive in other ways, but it is a force for innovation and efficiency economically. It is also superior to other authoritarian regimes (India is the most common example) because it is relatively responsive to crisis and the population. In neither case is there any reference to the organizational and cultural legacies of the revolution—whether with regard to repressiveness or responsiveness. There is no hint either that legacies of the revolution, however, weakened, may still be powerful ideological forces in shaping both people's demands and leaders' responses. Little noticed also is the continued anxiety about self-reliance and autonomy in the midst of participation in a neo-liberal global capitalist economy of which the PRC has become an integral part. The model appears as just a more efficient authoritarianism of uncertain origin. It is more common than not these days to find the explanation in the pre-revolutionary past, most importantly Confucianism of both state and people. In the end, what remains of a "Chinese model" open to emulation by others are authoritarianism, organizational efficiency, and innovativeness (or, more accurately, a willingness to experiment with different models of development).

What is glossed over are the social goals that theoretically continue to be an important constituent of the model, or the paradigm, as I suggest. A good part of the responsibility for this "forgetfulness" rests with PRC leaders and theorists who have been anxious to turn their backs on the revolutionary legacies to which they are heirs. The path of development since the launching of the "reforms" also has produced inequalities that easily create the impression that the revolutionary past is no longer relevant to understanding the present. PRC corporations are as ruthless as any of their capitalist competitors, if not more so, earlier promotion of national liberation struggles around the world has been replaced by full participation in power plays for participation in the capitalist world system, and the repressive response to popular dissatisfaction internally smacks more of efforts to sustain the power of the Communist Party than of any moves toward socialist equality and democracy. It is arguable, nevertheless, that unlike many foreign commentators anxious to pinpoint the sources of PRC success so as to emulate it or to partake of its benefits, a keen sense of the past as burden or inspiration continues to distinguish Chinese from foreign notions of a "model." Officially, at least, the reforms represent the latest of the series of experiments in the search for national autonomy, and national wealth and power, that have marked the history of modern China.

The Appeals of the Model

Among the competing "models" of a post-Eurocentric global modernity, the Chinese model receives the greatest attention because of the enormous economic achievements of the last two decades. It is also the one that is tacitly or explicitly contrasted with the US economy in its resonance with the "Beijing consensus" idea set against the neo-liberal "Washington consensus." There is some sense that as the Chinese economy overtakes its rivals, the model, too, may achieve global hegemony.

Despite its haphazard origins, the ascendancy of the Chinese Model in global development discourse is not entirely spontaneous. The idea has been the subject of ideological activity openly propagated by official propaganda organs at least since 2009, as the regime has raised its sights as a possible contender for world leadership. The activity has drawn further impetus from the regime's relatively successful weathering of the global recession of 2008–2009, as well as the elevation of the PRC GDP over that of Japan to the second spot in the world economy (we may ignore here the numbers game that makes it into the largest economy). It has benefited enormously in plausibility from the attention brought to the PRC by the 2008 Beijing Olympics and the 2010 Shanghai Expo. The activity is a key element in PRC's challenge to the US for world leadership. Its timing could not be better as the US economy continues to totter on the brink of another recession, the country suffers materially, morally and intellectually from the ill-conceived warfare in which it is mired, and the population is increasingly demoralized by a seemingly bleak future— which contrasts with the optimism of the majority of the Chinese population despite serious problems, ongoing repression of dissent, and widening social inequality.

The contrast also offers some explanation why the image the regime seeks to project as an alternative to US hegemony falls on receptive ears in many quarters across the globe. Unlike during the Cold War, when the contention over hegemony was fueled by serious ideological difference between capitalism and socialism, however truncated, the struggle over hegemony this time around is for supremacy within global capitalism: the neo-liberal capitalism of the "Washington consensus" and a state-managed and regulated capitalism represented by the so-called "Beijing consensus." The juxtaposition is valid but somewhat misleading. The PRC economy is state-managed, to be sure, and direct state involvement in the economy is one of its outstanding features. But it also has nourished off globalization, and the PRC regime since the mid-1990s has been a major proponent of the globalization of markets and production. What characterizes the PRC economy is a successful combination of authoritarian management internally with effective activity in the neo-liberal market. The combination was not of its invention, as it was characteristic of the neo-authoritarian economies to which I have referred above. But the Communist regime has been particularly successful in managing globalization while at the same time retaining strict control over the national market. A recent discussion by Stefan Halper observes that:

> today's emerging markets are increasingly drawn to a new and compelling doctrine of state-managed capitalism. They are learning to combine market

economics with traditional autocratic or semiautocratic politics in a process that signals an intellectual rejection of the Western economic model. According to this doctrine, the government maintains control over a partly liberalized economy and the people accept a very non-Western kind of civic bargain: political oppression in the public square in return for relative economic freedom and a rising quality of life. Both of these trends have a powerful cheerleader in Beijing.

We might add that it is not only in emerging economies that the model is viewed with interest. "The rejection of the Western economic model," itself hardly singular, has not stood in the way of "Western" corporations rushing to ingratiate themselves with the regime in order to gain access to the growing PRC market. While there are echoes in the current rush to the PRC of earlier myths of a boundless China market, the stakes this time around appear to be real enough to give plausibility to promises of the model. I underline the "appear," because while the growth of the PRC's economy is indisputable, how much of it may be shared with outsiders remains problematic. Observers have noted the exploitative conditions that limit access to the imagined riches of the PRC economy, most importantly in the joint enterprises that guarantee technology transfers to while strictly regulating the shares that accrue to the foreign partners. Some analysts go so far as to suggest that the PRC economy is only partially "globalized," with a "protectionist wall" jealously guarding "the 'state-owned' economy 'inside the system'" that is the backbone of the economy and the source of Party/state power.

Criticism of the PRC regime for its failures to live up to the demands of neo-liberal globalization may be justifiable from a legalistic perspective, but it is widely off the mark in terms of global power politics. How to participate in the global capitalist economy without yielding national sovereignty and autonomy has been an obsessive concern of Chinese radicals since the early twentieth century. The PRC's pursuit of national interest in a global economy may not be to the liking of the older centers of hegemony who had expected globalization to further enhance and broaden their hegemony. It makes perfect sense from a Chinese perspective. Unlike Mao-era anti-imperialism that demanded withdrawal from global capitalism, reform era "opening" of the national economy has sought to turn the tables on imperialism by exploiting the global economy in the service of national ends. The success with which the PRC regime has accomplished this goal is a major source of attraction in the Global South. Among those who have been subjected to two centuries of imperialist abuse and exploitation, and in the eyes of the majority of the PRC population, the benefits these successful policies have brought outweighs the regime's limitations of citizens' rights, its transgressions against human rights, and even the inequalities it has created in achieving national ends. From these perspectives, authoritarianism seems a small price to pay for achieving long-standing aspirations—especially among those who do not share in the basic assumptions of Euro/American democracy, or perceive it with good justification as an instrument of hegemony rather than liberation.

In a somewhat different register, there is little sign that evidence of serious problems in PRC's development has done anything to cool off the China fever. It is widely known in the PRC and abroad that the Party elite has used its political power to appropriate public wealth, and created inequalities that belie its socialist professions. Inequality is a major problem, but it is systemic corruption rather than inequality itself that is the greatest source of dissatisfaction among the public at large, and the underlying cause of daily protest against the regime. Party/state control of the economy in the name of national autonomy "disguises the privatization of state assets" which have been "carved up by PRC's rulers, their families and retainers, who are all in business for themselves." It would be unfair to compare the contemporary regime with prerevolutionary militarists, but there is some resemblance in its identification of national autonomy and welfare with its own progressively privatized interests. Where power is concerned, the important difference is in size and organizational reach which renders it into a dominant "public sphere" of its own, with the credibility and power to shape the course of the nation in the interest of its stakeholders much more efficiently than its military predecessors, or in more open societies. The confounding of the private and the public does give a new meaning to the old slogan that "without the Communist Party, there can be no new China"—as many in the PRC are quite aware, even though the news travels mostly by gossip.

The plunder of public wealth has been accompanied by investment in a greedy strategy of development—or, better still, maldevelopment—that is environmentally and socially destructive. Whether or not this development may be sustainable is quite uncertain, and the subject of ongoing speculation in the PRC and abroad. This uncertainty, the corruption, and the repressive apparatus that has been mobilized to keep the lid on popular discontent, are surely integral to any notion of a "Chinese model," and yet when they receive honorable mention, more often than not they are quickly dissolved into enthusiasm over the Chinese "miracle," the most impressive and momentous of the "miracles" that have characterized Eastern Asian development over the last half century. The teleology derived from these earlier miracles also provides the basis for predictions among foreign promoters that sooner or later the less desirable aspects of the model will fade away as a developing China inevitably moves toward greater democracy and public accountability. Future promise is enough to drive away any qualms about present ills.

Problems in the PRC's development may be easy to overlook when plunder of public resources, corruption, inequality, environmental destruction and repression have become norms of the global economy. Vague references to a rising "middle class"—more properly described as a "consuming class"—also disguise the enormous class differences within "the middle class." But there, too, the emergence of a wealthy ruling elite does not seem particularly out of the ordinary against the background of a transnational concentration of wealth and power from the least to the most developed societies.

Still, there is something remarkable about Euro/American corporations' ready, and seemingly enthusiastic, compliance with the authoritarian dictates of a state-managed economy of which systemic corruption is an integral ingredient. It is no surprise that inherently amoral elitist purveyors of luxury goods and services from manufacturers of high-end cars and yachts to exclusive makers of jewelry and perfume should seek to get in on the PRC market, and add the aura of their glamour to the newly wealthy elite. But so do the Rolling Stones and Bob Dylan, not to speak of countless corporations large and small for which the PRC has become the new economic frontier that in turn bestows prestige on those allowed to share in its riches. Mark Zuckerberg of Facebook fame has outstripped the competition by flaunting his conversion to Xi Jinping's version of "socialism with Chinese characteristics." Monetary gain and fear of being excluded from a growing market are no doubt very important factors in such compliance. Self-serving though it is, the argument that involvement in the PRC's economy will in the long-run help iron out problems of development is not to be dismissed offhand. But the complicity also suggests ideological resonance between the authoritarian neo-liberalism of the PRC regime, and the anti-democratic authoritarian premises of corporate organization that goes hand in hand with their global neo-liberalism.

The rush to the PRC has brought out into the open the incipient authoritarianism of global corporations as well as of the educational institutions entrusted with the intellectual, cultural and social preservation and propagation of democracy and the public good. Business corporations are not alone in giving ideological cover to the authoritarian practices of the PRC regime. More effective in prestige because of their claims to intellectual and ethical purity may be the cover afforded by educational institutions, which are increasingly allied with business interests, and behave like businesses themselves. North American, European and Australian higher education institutions are as eager as any business to establish "joint-enterprises" in the PRC. On the home front, they welcome with a mixture of cultural and economic anticipation the so-called Confucius Institutes, grassroots propaganda organs of the state, with seeming obliviousness to the

oppressive activities of the same propaganda establishment in the PRC in suppressing intellectual and political dissent—which is carried to campuses abroad in
efforts to discourage or even suppress discussion of
issues the PRC deems controversial. Faculty and
students who readily protest government involvement
on university campuses in the US appear to be mostly
silent when it comes to these institutions that arrive
with promises of language, culture, and business ties.
On occasion, they sink to depths of shameless servility
in their importunate appeal to PRC largesse. We may
recall here the extravagant praise College Board
President David Coleman heaped on the Hanban,
already cited in the Introduction: "Hanban is just like
the sun. It lights the path to develop Chinese teaching
in the U.S...The College Board is the moon. I am so
honored to reflect the light that we've gotten from
Hanban."

Contrary to those who are convinced that
economic development and new middle-class values
must inevitably usher democracy in their wake, there is
no reason to think on the basis of available evidence
that authoritarianism is inconsistent with a neo-liberal
global economy. Indeed, it may be quite the reverse:
what is at risk is not authoritarianism but democracy,
and the public good, as economic imperatives gain
ascendancy in global competition for resources, and
economic and political supremacy. To listen to US
political leaders, including President Obama who
surely knows much better, the goal of democracy is
most importantly to foster technological innovation.
The leaders of the PRC would have no problems agree-
ing with that one.

Despite brave talk about democracy, authoritarianism is more necessary than ever to keep in check

popular frustration with the inequalities that globalization has produced, not just in the PRC but globally. If the PRC's development has given it a new respectability, it is by no means an exclusive "Chinese" characteristic. What Stefan Halper describes as "the China effect" is real enough, but it is misleading to focus one-sidedly on the PRC's policies, and ignore the part global corporations and educational institutions play in sustaining authoritarianism even as they nourish off and deepen inequalities in the emergent reconfiguration of the world system.

Given the strategically crucial role the PRC has come to play in the global economy, the idea of a Chinese model as it is framed in most discussions articulates fundamental contradictions of global capitalism. The self-serving claim cited above that the Chinese model is superior not only to contemporary alternatives but even to the economies that initiated global economic modernization is to be approached critically because of its obliviousness to historical circumstances, as well to problems that await solution that are the products of development. Judging by railroads and automobiles, the PRC is a society on the move, which contrasts sharply with stagnation elsewhere. But the problems are equally impressive: unprecedented social and spatial inequalities resulting from development over the last three decades, reversing the achievements of the revolution, enormous ecological problems that threaten further development, corruption, social instability arising from these problems, and a deficit of human rights and democracy, however conceived, along with issues of free speech and legal due process. These, too, are products of the so-called China Model. A recent discussion refers to the PRC as "the world's first rich-poor country," with a GDP that is ranked #2 in the world, and a per capita GDP that ranks some-where around #90, depending on the source. The gap between the two rankings may serve as a measure of severe social and regional inequality that is easily over-looked in the rush to partake of "the deep wallet" of a dictatorial regime, and a new adoration for the unscrupulous Chinese elite as consumers of luxury goods. With severe inequality as a global condition, what attracts the greatest attention is the seemingly superior performance of the PRC national economy. How this performance may be sustained nevertheless presents serious questions.

Above all, however, is the question of the direc-tion of development, which is another crucial aspect of the notion of an "alternative." The PRC's develop-mental success has been achieved within the parameters set by existing models of development, most impor-tantly in the US, with a heavy emphasis on urbaniza-tion, the provision of consumer goods internally and externally, and a corresponding concentration of resources. While it is widely recognized that such a model of development may not be any more sustain-able in the PRC than in the United States, so far the corrections to it seem to have been mostly of a cosmetic nature. The destruction of the countryside and the depletion of natural resources continue apace. So do reliance on real estate speculation and automo-bile manufacturing to keep the engine of growth in motion. These are problems readily acknowledged by the leadership, and yet there is no plausible "alterna-tive" in sight.

It seems premature to speak of a Chinese model until these problems have been resolved, let alone a model as a socialist society. It also seems that those abroad who are most taken with the "Chinese model" are those who place economic and technological development ahead of all other social and political concerns, admirers of authoritarianism seeking escape from the problems of democratic societies, or, simply groupies of China cultivated by Confucius Institutes who seem to perceive China as a mélange of an exotic but suddenly accessible culture and much needed commercial opportunities for the future. The success of the PRC in alleviating poverty is a powerful source of attraction. So is the seeming vitality of the PRC society which disguises that it suffers from the same problems that afflict liberal corporate economies, especially problems of deep inequality, cultural disorientation, and ecology. PRC's problems are not exceptional. Currently available "models" all suffer from more or less similar problems which diminish their claims to serve as models for others. This is part of the crisis of our times. I think it is fair to say in the case of the PRC that however satisfying it may be from a nationalistic perspective, little of the admiration is fostered by hopes in movement toward socialist goals of social justice, equality, and democratic practices based on those ideals. The Chinese model in its success or as competitor can even be put to use in some advanced societies such as the US as an excuse for curtailing democracy and redirecting education toward corporate goals.

There is also a perception, that of a minority unfortunately, that if it is indeed possible to speak of a "Chinese model," it is as a model in the process of formation, a work in progress with a still uncertain future. It is quite obvious that even the PRC leadership is deeply divided over solutions to these problems, which are crucial to the formulation of development strategies. As is evident once again from the deep concerns of the Xi Jinping leadership, resolving the challenges of development, corruption and social inequality remains a priority. Whether or not these concerns in the long run overcome the fetishism of development, and redirect it toward socialist ends, remains an open question. Even if socialist policies are rejuvenated, moreover, questions will persist concerning their implementation over obstacles presented by conflicting economic and political interests. It is also important to remember that as times have changed, so has the understanding of socialism as necessarily people-based rather than state-centered. The Chinese Revolution of the twentieth century played an important part in placing some of these questions on the political agenda of Marxism and socialism. Whether or not they remain on the development agenda will have important consequences for the future.

Marxism, Capitalism, and The Chinese Model

I would like to conclude with a brief glance at Marxism in light of questions concerning the Chinese model. While the legacies of revolution and socialism are quite relevant to grasping the forces that continue to shape Chinese society and politics, it would be intellectually self-deceptive even for the Communist Party leadership to ignore that what most commentators in and out of China find attractive is not "socialism" but "capitalism with Chinese characteristics," made possible by repudiating the revolutionary socialism of the past. It takes considerable naivete, if not premeditated loss of vision, to remain blind to the disconnect between ideology, theory and practice that characterizes contemporary Chinese political, economic and social policies. Marxism is no more a concern for the population at large in China than it is elsewhere. On the other hand, depending on the political persuasion of the observer, the socialist professions of the regime continue to carry considerable weight in assessments of its weakness, or the hopes it offers as an alternative to actually existing capitalism.

Insistence on Marxism as a source of truth is obviously a condition of the Communist Party's legitimacy, as is its status as the political agent that has re-established national wealth and power. It is no less foolish to ignore the continued contribution of Marxism to the language of politics, moreover, than to disregard the revolutionary past as a storehouse of memories and policies that may be drawn upon to confront problems of the present when necessary. It is evidently the case, that rather than Marxism guiding policy, as the leadership would like to claim, it is the policy presently that shapes the contemporary interpretation of Marxism.

But Marxism may be relevant in unexpected ways to understanding the reasoning that underlies the idea of a Chinese Model that has deep roots in the Chinese Revolution.

Beginning in 2004, the leadership launched an effort to rejuvenate Marxism through the "Marxist Theoretical Research and Development Project" (literally, Basic Research and Construction, *Makesi zhuyi jichu yanjiu he jianshe gongcheng*), sponsored by President Hu Jintao himself. On the surface, at least, the rejuvenation of Marxism was intended to counter both developmentalism and consumerism by making human well-being the point of departure for and the end of development as demanded by socialist goals. Its most immediate goals could be seen as restoring ideological coherence to the Party organization, on the one hand, and to make sure, on the other hand, that the ideology was in conformity with the ideological lineage established by the leadership over the last thirty years: Marxism-Leninism—Mao Zedong Thought—Deng Xiaoping Theory—"Three Represents Theory" of Jiang Zemin—and Hu's own "Scientific Outlook on Development" (we would now add Xi Jinping's "China Dream"). The overarching goal of the project was to formulate a Marxism appropriate to China's development in a global age, based upon direct confrontation of the classical texts of Marxism, unmediated by other post-Marx/Engels/Lenin interpretations. Earlier efforts to make Marxism Chinese, most prominently under Mao in the 1940s, had sought to build upon Soviet Marxism. This time around, the interpretation was to be based on the Chinese experience of revolution and development.

The Project's stress has been on the exploration of what Marxist Classics had to say about socialist construction, rather than revolution, which had been the primary focus in the past. When it was initiated, it was assigned five tasks: to strengthen study of the "sinicization of Marxism" in Mao Zedong Thought, Deng Xiaoping Theory, and the "Three Represents"; re-translate and explain Marxist classics, establish a Marxist system appropriate to the times; produce higher education texts in political economy, philosophy, etc. with Marxist characteristics, as well as texts on modern history, etc., imbued with the spirit of Mao Zedong Thought, Deng Xiaoping Theory, and "Three Represents"; create new institutions of Marxist Research. The latter included the establishment of a new Marxism Research Institute in the Chinese Academy of Social Sciences. The Project itself involved, in addition to the Compilation and Translation Bureau and Marxist Research Institutes, University Departments as well as Party Schools across the country. One aspect of the project was to cull from the works of Marx and Engels the meaning they had assigned to a selected list of eighteen terms and concepts that are worth noting here because they are revealing of current concerns: democracy and political civilization; capitalism, socialism and communism; social development; agriculture and peasants; social development in economically and culturally backward societies; problems of globalization and "epoch" (*shidai*); ownership and distribution; political parties; war and peace; labor theory of value and surplus value; class, class struggle, proletarian revolution and dictatorship; religion; nationality (*minzu*); ideology, progressive culture and morality; human (*ren*); dialectical and historical materialism); principles of political economy; military.

Theoretical workers in the Party have been engaged in recent years in a global search in Marx-

Engels archives for published and unpublished materials that might offer textual alibi for the theoretical correctness of China's development under the reform regime. There is no reason to assume homogeneity of interpretation among the various institutions involved or their research staff from different backgrounds who themselves are not necessarily of one mind in evaluating contemporary development. But judging by the published output that has become available so far, the project has generated a Marxism that goes beyond Mao Zedong Thought in its nativist equation of Chinese Marxism with "the practice of the Chinese revolution." Indeed, some supposedly theoretical texts read very much like histories of the revolution from Mao to the present. Unlike in revolutionary days, moreover, when past philosophical legacies were viewed at least formally as objects of radical transformation in keeping with Marxist theoretical and historical assumptions, there has been some attempt to discover commonalities between Marxism and native legacies.

There is more at work here than the obvious, and perhaps trivial, point that Marxism has come to serve more explicitly than ever before as an instrument of national policy. The more important point is that the instrument, in the status of scientific universality ascribed to it, provides connections across national boundaries that endow the Chinese experience with global relevance. The temporal overlap between the Marxism project and the official dissemination of the Chinese Model may not be coincidental. Whether or not so intended by its promoters, there is an unmistakable dialectical interplay between the two projects which may be captured best by the philosophical notion of a "concrete universal," where the universal may be grasped only in its particular, overdetermined historicity. The Chinese model or better still, the Chinese example, may then be grasped as the singularly historical practice of universal principles that is open to emulation not as a universal pattern but for its procedures in articulating the universal to concrete historical circumstances (or vice versa, to be more consistently dialectical).

What is important here is overcoming the categorical formalism that has characterized discussions of Chinese development, and attending more closely to the thinking that guides change. Structural transformations after 1978 ("reform and opening") within the spatial context of Eastern Asia have been of the utmost importance in directing the trajectory that changes in China have followed. But these transformations are grasped best when viewed within the perspective of a longer stretch of time that encompasses the revolutionary period before and after 1949—which, after all, is merely a lifetime for some who have played key parts in both revolution and reform. Closer attention to these structural and historical circumstances might offer better clues to Chinese thinking on change than endless chase after fluid particulars, search for principles that transcend the limitations of time and place, or speculative meanderings in a "Chinese" or East Asian "mind." On the other hand, rather than take the idea of a "Chinese model" for granted, we need to be closely attentive to its entanglement in discourses on global power in which it has its inspiration, and from which it derives its significance and vitality.

III

Social Justice, Democracy and the Politics of Development: The People's Republic of China in Global Perspective[1]

Contemporary media reporting on questions of repression and dissent in the People's Republic of China, backed by expert voices of various kinds, is likely to yield a strong impression that at the heart of the problem is the continued hold on power of a dictatorial Communist Party riddled with factionalism and corruption. The diagnosis also casts a shadow on the revolutionary history that brought the Party to power. References to Mao Zedong's legacies target him as the ancestral source of contemporary problems. Given the Party's Leninist origins and constitution, however, the communism it claims as its guiding ideology—tinged with residual influences from the imperial past—must ultimately bear responsibility for its behavior. It follows from this line of thinking that as the revolution fades with development within the parameters of the capitalist

[1] This essay was co-authored with Roxann Prazniak. I am grateful to her for allowing me to include it here.

world-system, some of these problems will inevitably fade away. At the very least, development will foster a new democratic constituency, often equated with a vaguely defined rising "middle" class, that will push the Communist Party toward more democratic ways of governing. In the meantime, dissidents within and forces of democracy abroad are gradually nudging the Communist Party in that direction.

Plausible as this narrative sounds in light of the ongoing struggle of PRC intellectuals and working people for greater freedoms, democracy and justice, its teleological thrust is based on assumptions that call for closer scrutiny. Its plausibility rests, on the one hand, on the Party's repudiation of the "leftist" legacies of the revolution that led to unnecessary economic and social adventurism, and, on the other hand, its willingness to permit ideological and political discussion that would have been unimaginable during the heyday of revolution under Mao. Since 1978, the Party has sought to avoid repetition of the arbitrary exercise of leadership prerogatives during the Cultural Revolution by greater stress on rules, collective leadership and inner-Party democracy. At the same time, participation in the global economy has called for the establishment of a legal order that at least in theory is based on international norms. Development policies bank heavily internally on willing participation of the educated, reversing Cultural Revolution privileging of "redness" over expertise. The freedoms extended to society in order to secure such participation are very real indeed.

On the other hand, these changes have empowered dissidents to expand "the realm of freedom," and to hold the Party to its promise of a legal order, which is perhaps the most prominent theme of dissent in contemporary PRC. Dissent is further substantiated by the urban constituencies that have benefited from "reform and opening," who most likely would not object to the extension into the realm of politics of the freedom to consume that development has brought about—and is premised upon. There is no denying the ferment over these issues among the so-called "netizens." At least on the surface, the PRC shows every sign that with the deepening of development, it will follow the example of other authoritarian regimes, especially in Eastern Asia, in making the transition from dictatorship to democracy. The victory of capitalism over socialism in the Cold War provides historical confirmation to the persuasiveness of this narrative.

And yet, it is not at all certain that these changes justify the teleological hopes invested in them, which call for closer scrutiny. This is the purpose of the discussion below. We take up three questions that seem to be of particular significance but seldom are raised in evaluations of change in the PRC. First is the relationship to the legacies of the revolution of the Party and the people at large, including many dissidents, which is hardly the one-dimensional relationship it is often assumed to be. Second is the relationship of questions of repression and dissent in the PRC to its structural context within global capitalism. The PRC presently suffers from severe economic and social inequality that may be sustained only by political repression. It is frequently overlooked, however, that economic and social inequality are products of the very development policies for which the PRC is widely admired. The ironic consequence is that criticism directed at the PRC for its democratic deficit is more than compensated for by pressures to keep up a pattern and pace of development that gives priority to its functioning within the global system over the economic and political welfare of the population. Indeed, the "China Model" has more than a few admirers who look to it with envy against the "inefficiencies" thrown up by popular pursuit of justice in democratic societies. Deepening inequality is a pervasive phenomenon of global neoliberalism, of which the PRC is an integral part. Around the globe the predicament of democracy has set off a dialectic of protest and repression that has further thrown its future into jeopardy in any but a formal sense. Within a global context in which democracy is at risk and human rights in shambles, what does it mean for the PRC to be moving toward a more democratic regime? This being the case, finally, is there a case to be made that the PRC is better off exploring socialist alternatives in economy, society and politics than emulating models whose future is very much in question, in which case critique should be directed at holding the Party to its promise of socialism rather than its failures to live up to the examples of those who themselves are in retreat from democracy?

Protest and Repression

Before proceeding with an analysis of the questions above, it may be useful to summarize briefly the problem of repression and dissent in the PRC, which is somewhat more complicated than appears at first sight. Indeed, these terms are insufficient to encompass fundamental aspects of the relationship of the Party-state to its citizens.

The terms may serve well in reference to disagreements within the Communist Party, or even the cases of high-profile intellectuals and their associates and supporters. But they fall somewhat short of grasping the situation even in these cases in light of the display of lawless behavior by the state authorities. Despite state pretensions to legality, the "crimes" for which intellectuals such as Ai Weiwei, Chen Guangcheng, Liu Xioabo, and Ilham Tohti have been harassed, condemned, incarcerated and tortured (sometimes to death, as in the recent case of Li Wangyang), do not go beyond testing the limits of restrictive laws and even greater restrictiveness in their application. Restrictions on speech supposedly guaranteed by the PRC's own constitution are routine practice. Unemployed peasant workers are employed by the authorities to provide round-the-clock surveillance of victims whose only crime is to transgress against what the authorities deem the limits of speech or to pursue justice in the courts. The Party does not hesitate to resort to thuggery in order to enforce arbitrary restrictions. It is little wonder that the internal security budget of the PRC is larger than its defense budget.

In the case of minority populations such as the Tibetans, Uighurs and Mongolians, it is more proper to speak of seething rebellion, which the Party-state counters with what may best be described as colonial policies, both violent and non-violent. Non-violent means include most prominently the actual physical colonization of Tibet and Xinjiang by Han ethnicities from the interior, compounded with slow but inexorable extinction of local cultures. Violent means include erasure of physical and cultural legacies from the destruction of cities in the name of urban progress to prohibitions on religious practices which constitute the cultural fabric of these societies. At the extreme, the state has responded with fatal physical violence and incarcerations to overt expressions of rebellion against its rule. These may also serve as warnings to those harboring separatist sentiments in the neighboring societies of Taiwan and Hong Kong. The PRC all along has responded to calls for Taiwan independence with threats of forceful occupation. In Hong Kong, a Special Administrative Region ruled by and for business interests entangled in the PRC economy, the Beijing government's silent invasion is most evident in the increasing self-censorship of the press. Still, the relationship is on occasion a tense one as Hong Kong'ers continue to struggle for the preservation of their local rights, as well as the restoration of those of their compatriots across the border.

Possibly most fundamental in terms of the number of lives it touches and the structural inequalities it expresses is the disturbed relationship of the Party-state to the working population, especially the agrarian working population. An urban vision against the earlier Maoist glorification of the peasantry and practical necessities of capital accumulation have combined in a development policy that owes much of its success to dispossession of the agrarian population and the exploitation of agrarian labor driven off agriculture—the so-called "peasant-workers" (*nongmingong*). The exploitation of agrarian resources and labor was severe under Mao's leadership as well, but this time around the returns have been plundered by the ruling elite, mostly from the Party or with Party connections, that has produced one of the most unequal societies in the world. Conflicts over illegal or unjust confiscations of land by local cadres are at the source of the majority of the disturbances that numbered close 200, 000 last year. Villages have been emptied out of their young men and women, leaving behind the elderly and the very young, severely affecting family structures. The 150-200 million estimated migrant population of workers not only are treated like "illegal" migrants in being deprived of access to city amenities (including education and health), but are also a source of friction among the population because of ethnic and place differences. Depending upon the constitution of the migrant workers at any one place, gender and ethnic tensions are added to the class oppression and exploitation that has been a motor force of the PRC's development over the last two decades. With rare exceptions, the Party-state responds to expressions of popular unrest with further suppression and, when necessary, violence.

There are, of course, many satisfied with their improved lot since 1978. A recent study based on research conducted nearly a decade ago found that the majority were satisfied with the regime, and few harbored rebellious sentiments against it or the dominant urban class society over which it presides. The outstanding resentment was not of social difference but corrupt and ill-gotten gain. On the other hand, it is equally evident that violence or the threat of it is integral to the political and ideological structure of Chinese society.

Equally importantly, the question of dissent covers a broad spectrum: from liberal aspirations to a democracy similar to those of other advanced societies to the defense of legal rights, intellectual freedom and the pursuit of justice (if not equality) within the existing system to anti-colonial struggles for autonomy among minority peoples, and the struggles for autonomy and democracy in Hong Kong. If these struggles share one thing in common, it is the demand upon the Party-state for greater openness and respect for laws. Otherwise, they are also at odds with one another in their various causes with divisive consequences. It would be difficult if not impossible to find even on the left many who would condone greater autonomy to Tibet and Xinjiang, or letting go of Taiwan or Hong Kong.

It may be suggested that there is both too much criticism of the PRC, and too little. Criticism that focuses on the particularities of the PRC—the Communist regime—is more often than not off the mark in its Cold-War style juxtaposition of communism and democracy (or liberalism), as well as smoothing over evidence that the two terms of the juxtaposition may carry different weight and ideological baggage from different perspectives that are not just cultural but deeply political. It is probably safe to say that most Chinese conceive of democracy differently than it is typically understood in mainstream European and North American thinking as a strictly political issue, insisting on the inclusion of economic rights in any serious practice of democracy. They also have a different relationship to communism as part of their history. The juxtaposition also ignores a world-wide surge of oppressive practices of surveillance and criminalization of populations that may reveal PRC practices to be less peculiar to a "socialist" regime than appears superficially.

On the other hand, criticism of the PRC seems perfunctory when compared to threats of embargoes and wars against comparable dictatorial regimes. Power relations, economic interests, and a longstanding culturalist fascination with China combine to set China apart from other such regimes. Indeed, there has been an ongoing celebration of the PRC's development under the leadership of the Communist Party that recalls memories of the *Chinoiserie* that took Europe by storm three centuries ago. There are even displays of willingness to complicity with the regime's pursuit of global hegemony, most notoriously through the so-called Confucius Institutes. Not only governments and business but even educational institutions supposedly dedicated to critical inquiry are anxious to court a regime which is by common acknowledgment suspicious of free inquiry beyond its control. Rarely is this contradiction questioned. Business is less than eager to jeopardize its chances in the "China market" in the name of human or political rights. There are suggestions of envy in praises of a "China model" that has "successfully" combined neoliberal economic policies with authoritarian politics and social policy. New York University may offer the blatant example of this contradiction in its offer of an educational home to exiled dissident Chen Guangcheng (if briefly) even as it was in the process of building a campus in Shanghai.

Under the circumstances, it seems quite irrelevant to hold the Communist regime to its socialist promises and professions of Marxism. Critics are not interested in those "dead" issues. They are also justifiably skeptical about the socialist professions of a communist party which better answers to the description of "red capitalist" than socialist in any serious sense of that term These issues, however, are of the utmost significance to the regime and many of its subjects—especially the intellectuals—and they are also divisive for both the Party and dissidents aligned against it, who also dissent with one another over them. Dissent, in other words, is not just a matter of democracy and communism but shares in all the complexities of Chinese politics.

The Past in the Present

The legacies of the revolution and Bolshevik structure of the Communist Party are no doubt important elements in structuring Chinese politics. On the other hand, it needs to be kept in mind that what might be a necessity of revolutionary politics aimed at social transformation can easily degenerate into garden variety dictatorship designed to protect organizational and class interests. PRC politics presently partakes of both these elements. Increasingly, however, legitimation is located not in the necessities of developing toward some social-ist vision but national goals of "wealth and power."

Critiques that presuppose the abandonment of the revolutionary past are in some ways widely off the mark. To be sure, Mao is condemned for his part in the Cultural Revolution, and the Party remains wary of any leftward turn in politics, as is attested by the Bo Xilai episode and the Chongqing experiment. Whether or not this means the abandonment or fading away of the revolution and Mao's legacies either for the Party or the population at large remains an open question. The Chongqing experiment was a far cry from the Cultural Revolution. It advocated closer political intervention in the economy to allocate a greater share of the returns to populist causes like affordable housing for the needy, especially for the rural population displaced by its own pursuit of development. It also revived some of the political and ideological themes of the Cultural Revolution that in theory were intended to alleviate some of the adverse social and cultural effects of capitalist development. But the experiment did not challenge immersion in global capitalism, which was a fundamental difference from the Cultural Revolution pursuit of nearly autarchic development. Aside from "gangsterism," its main target was to mitigate the class and urban-rural inequalities that are acknowledged by the Party leadership as fundamental problems. According to supporters on the left, some of whom were directly involved in the experiment, it was nevertheless a sufficient threat to the reigning neoliberal assumptions guiding the regime to invite quick suppression. Ongoing conflicts over how best to steer economic development toward national and social ends seem to have been exacerbated in this case by personal and factional ambitions and animosities. The suppression has hardly eliminated divisions within the Party over its relationship to its revolutionary past, as is indicated by recent calls for return to the policies of New Democracy, blending socialist and capitalist elements, that had brought the Party to power in 1949. The Cultural Revolution had been the negation of New Democracy. What they shared in common was a commitment to national ends.

It is often overlooked that what was repudiated after 1978 was neither the revolution nor Mao Zedong but Maoist policies of the Cultural Revolution from the mid-1950s to their reversal after 1978. In Party ideology, the essence of Mao Zedong Thought is identified as "making Marxism Chinese," of which the formulation of New Democracy in the 1940s was the foundational moment. Under Deng Xiaoping's leadership after 1978, the Party reaffirmed the correctness of New Democracy policies, and portrayed "socialism with Chinese characteristics" as further development of Mao Zedong Thought under new national and global circumstances. Even the radical departures under Deng's successors (Jiang Zemin, Hu Jintao and Xi Jinping) are portrayed in official ideology as the unfolding of Mao Zedong Thought. Mao Zedong Thought has been stripped of its social revolutionary implications, and rendered into an ideology of national development. Accordingly, the century long revolutionary process itself has been revised to read as the "road to [national] rejuvenation" (*fuxingzhi lu*) as in the exhibit at the newly reorganized National History Museum.

While the preservation of Maoist revolutionary legacy is of obvious importance to the reaffirmation of the Communist Party's legitimacy, its significance goes beyond this legitimating function. The official "derevolutionization" of Mao does not rule out the possibility of the return of revolutionary policies if circumstances permit (or demand) it, which was the case with the Chongqing experiment. This possibility is not limited to the Party, or leftist intellectuals. Despite intense resentment in some quarters, Mao continues to command iconic status among the common people of China as a powerful symbol that can be mobilized against the turn the Party has taken. To the chagrin of the leadership, peasants in the 1990s built temples to Mao Zedong, surpassing his metaphorical deification during the Cultural Revolution—coincident with the "Mao fever" evoked by the hundredth anniversary of Mao's birth in 1993, but more importantly with the full scale turn to capitalism after 1992 which initiated a process of dispossessing the common people. While such displays were quickly suppressed, the themes associated with them remain alive even when they are not explicitly attached to Mao's person or invoke revolutionary precedents. Peasants may have longer memories stored in their stories than urban populations at the mercy of changing fashions. If revolution even under Mao did not eliminate their exploitation, it at the very least empowered them politically in unprecedented ways. Those memories have not disappeared. There is some evidence that protestors in the recent Wukan uprising in Guangdong invoked memories of the Hailufeng Soviet established in the same location in 1927 by the Communist intellectual Peng Pai. Just recently, in December 2014, the 121st anniversary of Mao's birth was celebrated with sacrifices to his memory.

Criticism that focuses on the legacies of revolution and socialism are misleading most egregiously in ignoring that it is not socialism but nationalism that accounts for the behavior of the regime. After all, the Chinese Revolution was a national revolution for autonomous development against "semi-colonialism," with socialism as its vehicle. The vehicle gave the nationalism its particular flavor, but with the retreat from any operative vision of socialism, the latter seems more than ever merely a front for the national pursuit of wealth and power under the leadership of the Communist Party. It is important to remember that most of the criticism directed against the PRC for its "socialist" failures overlooks the fundamental national interest that guides the Communist regime's domestic and foreign policies, including the repressive exploitation of its own population in the name of development and security.

Unless we take socialism to be the concentration of wealth and power in the Communist Party, there is little in "socialism with Chinese characteristics" that may be described as socialist in any strict sense of the term (we will return to this later). The legacies of revolution derive their vitality not from visions of socialism but from their roots in nationalism. For the population at large no less than the Communist Party as such, the revolution is inextricably entangled in the struggle for national autonomy and power. Nationalism is particularly virulent among "new left" intellectuals. While the Communist Party has repudiated the radical social, economic and political policies of the Cultural Revolution, the militant nationalism that the Cultural Revolution espoused would become even more indispensable to the regime in filling the ideological vacuum left by the abandonment of the socialist project after 1978 in mobilizing popular support for its policies. The so-called "new nationalism" after the 1990s owed much to the nationalist propaganda effort that accompanied the repudiation of militant socialism in the early 1980s, when nationalist literature addressed to various constituencies of the regime flooded the publishing market. Since then, the regime deliberately has fueled nationalism by playing up the "national humiliation" inflicted upon the country by imperialism since the middle of the nineteenth century which was overcome only by Communist victory in 1949. Overcoming national humiliation would seem to justify expansion over imagined "lost" areas, laying claims to territories or seas on the basis of manufactured historical and legal rights.

If there is anything novel about the effort, it is the use of nationalism to cover up the retreat from socialism. Resentment of "national humiliation" has been a driving force of revolution for the past century. Among the legacies of the Cultural Revolution is a militant nationalism that still lingers among the population at large. Indeed, over issues of national sovereignty, it is difficult to avoid the impression that it is public pressure on the Party that drives militancy than the other way around. Conflicts with neighboring states over disputed island territories or the Southeast Asian Sea invariably provokes furious reactions among "netizens" and even thoughtful intellectuals. There was considerable resentment against Liu Xiaobo for his suggestion that China might have been better off if it had gone through a phase of colonial rule (as in Hong Kong). While economic interests of the Party corporate elite are not to be ignored in the discriminatory policies against foreign enterprises, they are consistent with the search for economic autonomy that has been a concern of reformers and revolutionaries since the beginning of the nineteenth century. The expectation from "reform and opening" after 1978 and "globalization" since the 1990s was not relinquishing control over the national economy but to utilize these "tools" to achieve the long-desired goal of autonomous development—which has made the PRC attractive especially to societies of the Global South.

Judging by the surge of nationalism since the 1990s, development seems to have reinforced national pride and close-mindedness despite the cultural opening to the outside world, accompanied by enthusiastic consumption of things foreign and the rush to educational institutions abroad of the offspring of the new economic elite. To hear some Chinese intellectuals argue these days, one would think that the PRC's phenomenal development since the 1980s owes nothing to forces from the outside, including *huaren* overseas, but was the product of national virtues, often going past the revolution itself to vague claims about "traditional" values of one kind or another—echoing without acknowledgment arguments of modernization discourse. Such arguments, accompanied by claims to an "alternative modernity" (the China Model), also ignore the extent to which the PRC has mimicked development in other capitalist societies, especially the US, overtaking which seems to be a national obsession. Contemporary China is a laboratory case in the study of the dynamics of "Sino-centrism."

More to the point here, there is little reason to expect that this nationalism will fade away anytime soon. The hope that with development the socialist legacy will vanish into the past is largely misplaced because the issue is not socialism but this militant nationalism that has appropriated socialist policies for its own. Indeed, this nationalism derives new energy from development, and bolsters the regime's claims to the inextricable links between national salvation and its own preservation. Whether over greater independence for the minorities, or Taiwan independence in foreign relations, opening markets in its economic relations, or greater freedom and democracy internally, it is national security as perceived by a Party that is not only the political ruler of the country but increasingly the dominant social class as well that will determine future behavior.

The PRC in the Neoliberal World System

The second set of issues that call for closer scrutiny pertains to the PRC's context within global capitalism. Both state repression and popular struggles against it are no doubt deeply marked by "Chinese characteristics." Nevertheless, the most widespread causes of discontent—forceful expropriation of agricultural land, widespread dislocation of the population, severe exploitation of labor, social and spatial inequalities, corruption from the top to the bottom of the political structure, urban and rural pollution—are all entangled in the development policies that the PRC has pursued since the 1980s in its quest of "wealth and power" within the context of a neo-liberal global capitalism. Indeed, isolating questions of social conflict and state repression in the PRC from these entanglements more often than not leads to tendentious readings that blame the problem on local cadres or the nature of the political system. On the other hand, it obviates the need to explore further how successful and rapid incorporation in global capitalism has come to shape the dynamics of the system and the behavior of its various agents despite increasingly ineffective efforts on the part of the regime to shield society from the consequences of its own policies, which accounts for much of its repressive policies. It also renders opaque the part played by outsiders in Chinese politics, not just as agents of progress toward human rights and democracy, as some would naively believe, but also in their economic and ideological complicity with repressive policies.

The conversion of land into capital, the creation of a floating labor force available for this process, and the sale of cheap labor power to fuel an export-oriented economy are all aspects of capital accumulation within a globalized capitalist economy. If anything distinguishes the PRC, it is the presence of a sprawling organizational structure put in place by the revolution that has guaranteed the efficient performance of these processes, with coercion whenever necessary. This organization was created initially to achieve the twin tasks of economic development and social transformation in the creation of a socialist society, where in hindsight the task of social transformation inhibited full performance in the task of economic construction. Indeed, conflict between the two goals would lead to social tensions that exploded in the disastrous chaos of the Great Leap Forward, the Cultural Revolution and, in a much more limited scope, the Tiananmen tragedy of 1989.

The removal of the inhibitions with the move to a "socialist market economy" after 1978 would unleash the full economic potential of this organizational structure, but at a price: The conversion of a revolutionary party intended to pursue the cause of a just society into a "ruling party" representing "the most advanced social forces, technologies and culture"(the famed "three represents" of Jiang Zemin) devoted to the relentless pursuit of "wealth and power." This is not to suggest that a just society had been achieved before 1978. Even during the revolutionary years before 1976 "revolution" had been placed at the service of developmentalist goals of overtaking capitalist societies that justified the reorganization of society into more efficient units of production and the severe exploitation of labor under banners of revolution. Nevertheless, few would deny that these revolutionary slogans carried the weight they did because no one doubted the seriousness of the regime about the kind of society inscribed on the banners. This would change after the regime concluded from the Tiananmen upheaval, and Deng Xiaoping's personal testimonial to the success of the special economic zone in Shenzhen, that enrichment of the population was the best cure to excessive popular interest in politics. Incorporation in the global capitalist economy was achieved under Deng's successors under the sign of "globalization." This, however, made it more urgent than ever to guard national sovereignty, which may account for the surge of the so-called "new nationalism" in the 1990s.

There can be little question about the renewed dynamism these changes brought to the party and government organization, or the popular enterprise they stimulated—ironically, in hindsight, beginning with the agricultural population in the 1980s. The township enterprises flourishing from the late 1980s through the early 1990s represented successful efforts by local cadres who for a while were given considerable leeway in the pursuit of capital and the negotiation of development in their domains. "Globalization" of the economy from the late 1990s was accompanied by the re-centralization of decision-making, greater coordination of development, and the reassertion of the power over the economy of state-owned financial, energy and industrial enterprises.

Despite the ideological and organizational particularities of the PRC that are products of its revolutionary history, the accumulation of capital over the last three decades have been marked by class formations and relationships characteristic of the "primitive accumulation" of capital elsewhere. The distinction of the regime, derivative of its claims to socialism, is almost total control of resources, including labor, which under this "workers' state" is not allowed to represent itself because it is already represented by the "socialist" regime. One critic of the regime, Qin Hui, has ascribed China's rapid development to a "low human rights" regime. Domestic accumulation has been achieved through the conversion of land into capital, in the process releasing huge amounts of cheap and controlled labor-power that then was put to use in the construction of cities, infrastructure projects, and industries. This laboring population also provided the workers and large numbers of women in export production financed by foreign and domestic capital that would make China into the "factory of the world," and a major depository of global capital.

The PRC is an outstanding example of the private appropriation of public resources that David Harvey has described as "accumulation by dispossession." The Party's claims to be *the public* have grown less convincing over the years with increasing evidence of the private disposal of the country's wealth through party control of the economy. The new Chinese economic elite working through or with the Party does not differ much from its counterparts elsewhere in the unprecedented accumulation of wealth in the hands of a small minority of the population. The "blood-line" faction which has received much attention recently in connection with the Bo Xilai affair, and the prospective Party Chairman, Xi Jinping, goes so far as to claim special privileges for descendants of revolutionary party leaders that smacks of a new aristocratic formation in the making.

Rapid economic development has created an urban middle class that may be proof of developmental success. This "middle class" is probably better described as a "consuming class" that, like most consuming classes elsewhere, is less interested in political and cultural democracy than its freedom to consume. The regime can also boast that for all the problems of development, it has managed successfully to feed its huge population. But these successes barely disguise the lop-sidedness of the PRC's development, and the corruption it has unleashed, which are obviously matters of great concern to the leadership. Commanding the second largest economy in the world, the PRC nevertheless ranks among the world's poorest countries in terms of per capita GDP. Most of the wealth is concentrated in the hands of the top 20% of the population, but especially the top one percent. The rural population, which is still the majority, languishes as agriculture is commercialized, with increasing participation from agribusiness. In the meantime, the population is being crammed into "megacities" beset with problems of pollution, traffic, and the yet unpredictable toll on the population of life under such circumstances. The working population is still subject to abuse at the hands of domestic and foreign corporations. Workers fight back, needless to say, and the second generation of peasant-workers would seem to be less amenable to exploitation and prejudice than their parents. Aside from colonial policies in minority areas such as Tibet, Xinjiang and Mongolia (which constitute the larger part of the country's land mass), the repressive apparatus of the state is directed most assiduously to keeping under control, with violence if necessary, protests against inequality, exploitation, unjust plunder of public resources, rights to land in particular, and environmental pollution. State terrorism against these protests includes incarceration, torture and outright murder of their leaders, with similar treatment meted out to intellectuals and lawyers who throw in their lot with popular protests. Little wonder, as the Communist

Party is no longer just a political but also an economic entity which has a direct interest in the accumulation of capital. It has so far been more successful than its predecessors in the twentieth century in convincing the population that its interests are also the national interest, but how long it can do so is anybody's guess. One of the particularities of the PRC is that the organizational apparatus that has enabled its development is equally efficient as an instrument of repression so long as it retains its coherence, which it has done successfully so far through the distribution of economic rewards and privileges throughout the organization. We should remember that the Communist Party and its auxiliary organizations make up around 20 percent of the population.

Viewed through the prism of the primitive accumulation of capital within the context of global capitalism, the PRC's developmental trajectory invites a more sociological approach to questions of social protest and political repression. We may ask, for instance, whether in the expropriation of land rights, the concentration of wealth, the exploitation and mistreatment of labor, immense class, gender, ethnic and racial differences, and violent suppression of challenges to the status quo, the contemporary PRC might compare favorably with the United States in the second half of the 19th century—without even referring to civil war and the colonial abjection of the native population? How does the PRC compare in these regards with other contemporary societies embarked on "primitive accumulation," from Brazil and South Africa, to Turkey, Russia and India? Is the excessive preoccupation with repression in the PRC a function not of its record as such as it is of the greater visibility it has acquired on the world scene by virtue of successful economic development? On the other hand, this comparison also raises the question of whether or not the PRC may be able to follow the same trajectory as the United States earlier moving toward a more egalitarian and just society once done with the business of "primitive accumulation?" If that was possible at an earlier time, is it still possible under conditions of global capitalism?

We are not likely anytime soon to see headlines such as "The Chinese are using a more spare version of our tactics in eliminating the Indians," or "Chinese torture internal dissidents while the US concentrates mainly on foreign terrorists," or "Inequality and corruption in China reach US levels," or yet still, "Is the US moving toward authoritarian capitalism?" Professional codes and ideological blinders combine to drive away any such temptation.

The point of such questions is not to abolish distinctions between democratic capitalist societies and an authoritarian capitalism directed by an all-powerful party-state that is also heir to revolutionary repression now placed in the service of a new status quo. Nor is it to absolve Chinese political leaders of their responsibility for abuses of the citizenry, or to deny China's particular historical legacies. It is rather to point to the broader social and historical context of individual or regime responsibility, and to relocate problems of repression and protest in the structural dynamics of China's development. It is also to suggest that given the structural links between contemporary societies and the common political, economic and cultural forces that shape their actions, comparable tendencies may be observed globally, subject to local variation due to differences in historical legacies, social alignments, and political and ideological dispositions in different societies. If the PRC is having problems with democracy, inequality, political legitimacy, transgressions against citizens' and human rights, etc., so is the rest of the globe, including those who would claim universal values for their own. Differences in the magnitude of the problems and the means and capacity to deal with them should not be allowed to disguise these commonalities. The recognition of commonality also calls for a more complicated understanding of responsibility for these problems, which may appear in different guises in different societies but also articulate the contradictions of a global capitalism to which no outside exists except in its interior.

It is not possible to delve further into these questions here. But in general they cast the question of social conflict and repression in the PRC in a different light than when it is viewed in isolation. The first question may seem irrelevant in the contemporary world, but it is at least a caution against over-zealous self-righteousness in condemnations of the PRC. As for the other questions that are more contemporary in their presuppositions, it seems that the PRC's problems are shared to varying degrees in comparable societies, even though they find different outlets of expression depending on the openness of each political system to popular political participation. None matches the efficient ruthlessness of development in the PRC with power concentrated in the hands of the Communist Party. The speedy development for which the PRC is justly admired was made possible by the equally speedy exploitation of natural and social resources, which in its rapidity and deep social consequences has attracted attention globally. But the concentration of wealth in ever fewer hands, increasing inequality, the impoverishment of the middle strata of society, increased use of surveillance and outright disregard for previously recognized rights, and the effective disenfranchisement of populations are pervasive phenomena of global neoliberal capitalism not only in developing countries but developed ones as well.

This context has a bearing on the future direction of the PRC as well. Whether or not the PRC will follow the example of developed countries in gradually overcoming the adverse social and ecological consequences of "primitive accumulation," achieved with unprecedented rapidity. This might have seemed possible in an earlier time when the teleology of modernization was still plausible. It seems much less certain within the context of a global capitalism when the so-called developed countries are in retreat from a century of achievements in social welfare and justice, as well as a range of citizenship rights. There has been some redistribution of wealth globally, but what has resulted is a far cry from the promise in modernization discourse of one big "middle class" around the world, with attendant progress in institutions that guarantee social justice and democracy.

In such an environment, there are no clear guides to the future, which finds expression presently in claims to "alternative modernities," more often than not based on modernized cultural claims that seek to roll back ideas of social justice and democratic rights as they have been understood for two centuries under the regime of Euromodernity. There may be the promise here of a more cosmopolitan understanding of these ideas. It seems that more often than not, cultural claims serve as excuses for the perpetuation of authoritarian systems that accord with the interests of their hegemonic constituencies while denying to the people at large the political rights indispensable to the defense of their civil and social rights. This, too, has become a pervasive phenomenon of the contemporary world.

In other words, within the contemporary global system characterized by the concentration of wealth, the increased restriction of civil and social rights, cultural nationalist fragmentation, there is little reason for the leaders of the PRC to modify the repressiveness of the regime, except to correct the contradictions that obstruct further development. The apparent regression in the so-called advanced countries may serve as a negative example, a warning not to follow in their wake. Indeed, ideas of "the China model" or "the Beijing Consensus" that have attracted quite a bit of attention in global corporate circles and many governments suggest an envy for the authoritarian efficiency of the Chinese Party-state, ready to part with citizens' and human rights as obstacles to the efficient conduct of business. Similarly, in the name of closer cultural and economic relations with the PRC, educational institutions around the world (the majority in the US) have invited into their midst the so-called Confucius Institutes where behind the façade of the Hanban) the Wizard of Oz resides in the Central Propaganda Department. It is remarkable that the many China specialists involved in these institutions should not wonder publically why these institutes are named after a revered cultural and philosophical icon who remains suspect at home! Whatever the criticisms thrown at them from certain quarters, the PRC leadership has every reason to find vindication of its policies and legitimation of its developmental trajectory in its fetishization as a model, and the ready acquiescence of cultural institutions abroad with its propaganda goals.

A Socialist Regime?

At the root of problems of protest and repression is the frenetic development policies of the regime driven by multiple goals of advancing the power and standing of the nation, a genuine need to improve the lot of all Chinese, the interests of the Party-economic elite, popular demands of a moneyed class for more of the same, and global investors urging it on, not necessarily in that order. For all the talk about social reform and environmental regulation, cadres are evaluated for their economic performance, reinforcing local urges to plunder. Those closer to the center seem to have accumulated enormous wealth, usually through family members with falsified names. There is likely little distinction in the minds of this ruling class between its class interests and the interests of the nation and the population.

If we shift attention from high-profile intellectuals to the people at large, most protest in numbers and magnitude in the PRC come from the people at large, even without including the minority peoples. These protests also draw in intellectuals and activist lawyers as supporters or sympathizers, as is evidenced in the cases of Ai Weiwei and Chen Guangcheng, to mention two that have recently made the headlines. The plight of the people provided cover for the Chongqing experiment which, despite the factional intrigue that motivated it, revealed deep divisions within the Party on the best way to address accumulating social problems. The experiment ended in failure due to a number of reasons—from the sordid intrigues of the Bo family to its own internal contradictions and vigilant counter-pressures from neo-liberal forces in the Party. Despite the defeat, its revival of revolutionary themes should not be dismissed lightly. There are also examples in grassroots struggles, as in the case of Wukan in Guangdong where the locals have been struggling for the past five years against the expropriation of their land and the high-handed behavior of local officials—at a location that nearly ninety years earlier had been home to China's first Soviet government. Elsewhere, popular protest against environmental pollution has won victories in a number of locations.

These protests represent struggles against the injustices that have accompanied "development." The distinguished sociologist Sun Liping of Tsinghua University in Beijing has noted that of the estimated 180, 000 grassroots protests of various magnitude that took place in 2011, 65 percent had to do with land issues. Less salient but equally significant are strikes and other forms of protest by urban laborers, and environmental protests that cut across class and regional differences have been on the increase in response to the deepening crisis of pollution and ecological destruction. There has been ongoing protest against privilege and corruption, provoked by abusive and criminal behavior on the part of the political and economic elite. Despite some progress, however, the state still responds to these protests with repression. In the meantime, the returns from development are concentrated in the hands of a small elite serviced by mostly foreign purveyors of luxury living, with foreign passports ready in hand in case development runs into trouble. Corruption oils the wheels of development.

It is important to call upon the PRC regime to respect human and citizens' rights, and live up to its own laws. It is even more important to recognize that at the most fundamental social level, such calls are bound to be limited in effectiveness. What breeds state lawlessness and repression is not just the greed and corruption of individuals but the imperatives of development, or more accurately, a developmentalism that is oblivious to social and environmental costs so long as it contributes to national power and the class interests of the Party-state elites. It is also at this level that China's problems are inextricably entangled in global processes. To global corporations that benefit directly or indirectly from China's development the welfare of the Chinese population is at best a secondary concern. Educational institutions that increasingly behave as corporate enterprises appear quite satisfied to serve as fronts for Chinese propaganda so long as it brings with it possibilities of campus expansion, increased student enrollments, and perhaps business connections. And last, but not least, consumers around the world who must share in the responsibility for the social and environmental havoc that the PRC's development has wrought. Developmentalism itself is not a Chinese obsession but a driving force of global capitalism. The accumulation of wealth and power in the hands of a small elite is not just a Chinese but a global problem, cutting across distinctions of advanced, developing, and yet-to-develop societies. What distinguishes the PRC is the ruthless efficiency to achieve the speed with which it has been able to pursue development in the absence of democratic obstacles that have tempered the same tendencies in other "developing" societies. The ruthless elimination of popular opposition to its developmental policies is one of the foremost characteristics of "the China model" that has earned the PRC widespread admiration in corporate circles.

What sustains the increasingly untenable political structure in the PRC is not just the resilience of the system put in place by the revolution but global capital that has come to have a large stake in this system. If spokespeople for global capital are critical of the Chinese system, it is not because of its authoritarianism but because of its resistance to further opening its doors to capital (PRC spokespeople, interestingly, complain of reverse discrimination against *their* transnational corporations, which also happen to be owned by the state, further complicating matters). Global corporations, including the corporate university, that have become stakeholders in the PRC economy like to justify their involvement with the prospect that more intense engagement will bring greater democracy and human rights to China. There is scarce evidence for such hope in their home countries in Europe and North America in the increasing vulnerability of human and citizens' rights, as well as the debilitating consequences for academic security and freedom of the corporate and business assault on higher education.

The PRC needs a systemic shift, to be sure, but not of the kind proposed by global capital which in its accumulation of economic and political power has created the global class divisions that is at the source of these problems in China and elsewhere. The sociologist Sun Liping and his research team conclude that the concentration of economic and political power in the hands of the Party-state is responsible for the most fundamental ills of society, and is increasingly incapacitated by its interests in the system to do anything about the crisis. This situation, too, has parallels elsewhere in the world. It should come as no surprise to those involved in "the Arab Spring" of 1911, and the global Occupy movements that have been going on for over a year now without any foreseeable resolution of the problems that gave rise to them.

What Sun calls "social" or "political" decay is also characteristic of the current global situation in other major world economies. While different political and cultural legacies guide the trajectories of dissent and repression, societies globally are torn with class inequalities that the entrenched political and ideological orthodoxy refuses to acknowledge, a first step in the search for alternatives. In this regard there is little difference between a United States where party politics no longer expresses a democratic will but has become a mask covering the betrayal of democracy and popular welfare in the service of corporate and financial interests, and a PRC where socialism no longer serves as a guide to creating a different kind of society but instead serves as a cover for an authoritarian corporate capitalism. Contrary to apologists for authoritarian politics, the struggles over power and policy in the Communist Party do not seem to be any the less contentious in its power and policy politics than the cantankerous multiparty conflicts in the US. It is no doubt important that in an open society it is easier to bring problems out into the open if solutions are to be found, but so far immobility seems to characterize politics around the world as if there is a common reluctance to recognize the problems created by neoliberal globalization. It is not, therefore, very convincing that further opening China's doors to global capital will resolve the problems it faces. What is needed is another kind of change that shifts the focus from development that benefits global corporations and the global ruling class that controls them to a kind of development that can meet popular needs for welfare and justice and is attentive to ecological consequences—not in words but deeds.

Whether or not things fall apart before they take a turn for the better remains to be seen in the PRC as elsewhere. The fact that the Chongqing experiment failed due to apparently personal and institutional reasons should not blind us to its larger significance: the continued importance of the revolutionary past as a resource for solving contemporary problems. It is true that those resources have been compromised by their disastrous consequences in the past. But they retain considerable power in invoking a century of revolutionary quest for social justice and political sovereignty for the people at large that is yet to be fulfilled. The imagination of such a future presupposes breaking with an official vision that is postponed to a future so remote that it is meaningless. What makes a vision politically relevant is its immanence.

Is this a possibility in the PRC? Perhaps. Intensified repression has done little to stem protest activity which continues despite intensifying repression under the Xi regime, emboldened by a series of successful popular mobilizations one after another in Wukan, Dalian, and more recently, Shifang and Qidong. But the obstacles are formidable. For the time being, the leadership has decided on suppression of dissent rather than pursue any radical shift in direction despite its recognition of deep-seated problems. Social and political "decay," Sun Liping et al. suggest, is a major source of indecision. The Xi Jinping leadership has undertaken a double pronged attack on Party corruption, on the one hand, and on the other hand intellectual dissent and protest against Party rule. But the rulers, with an efficient organization at their disposal, remain resistant to change. Among the population at large, there is a considerable constituency that is satisfied with the system of which it is the product. For those who may not be happy with their lot, the promise of national progress and power is nevertheless a powerful substitute for personal fortunes, as likely to serve state purposes as to engage in social resistance to the state. Where issues of national sovereignty are concerned, popular nationalism is often more militant than that of the state. Indeed, recent cases where the word "traitor" has been bandied about suggest a readiness to foment a xenophobic nationalism against protests that draw upon "foreign" inspiration. The cultural nationalism that has been on the rise since the late 1980s has all the militant fervor of Mao-era nationalism against imperialism and global class divisions, but is directed now at cultural defiance of Euromodernity, stressing the particularity of Chinese identity even as China becomes an integral part of contemporary global capitalism and "Chinese culture" is dissolved into a consumer culture. For the left, it represents an effort to find an autonomous path of development. It is also a fertile breeding ground for xenophobic nativism.

Here, too, the PRC is at one with the world of global modernity which is the product of a fundamental contradiction between the globalization of capitalist modernity and the resurgence of cultural nationalism. One immediate consequence is the closer policing of culture, and those involved in cultural production. Cultural fragmentation also serves as an excuse for intensifying surveillance and police control in society, which are then extended across the breadth of society to turn into norms of everyday life. In the case of the PRC, there has been an intensification over the last two-three years of already quite intense practices (by world standards) of surveillance and repression.

One thing would seem to be certain: China's problems are the world's problems, and the world's problems are China's problems. Only if criticism takes this into account can it hope to point to solutions that go beyond surface phenomena to their systemic sources. Freedom and democracy are most important in opening the gates to exploration of problems of development and possible ways out of global modernity.

IV

Forget Tiananmen, You Don't Want to Hurt the Chinese People's Feelings—and Miss Out on the Business of the New 'New China'![2]

> I vividly recall the shrill voice of the announcer commenting on the scrawny youth standing in front of a column of tanks in Tiananmen Square on June 5, 1989: "If our tanks press forward," he asked, "would that pathetic low life really be able to halt their progress?" I was 15 at the time. "That's right!" I thought. "The soldiers were being truly merciful."
>
> —Murong Xuecun

Twenty-five years ago, in the early hours of June 4, the people's government in Beijing turned its guns on the people of the city who had risen in protests that spring to express their frustration with Party despotism and corruption. Students from Beijing universities held center stage in their occupation of Tiananmen Square. But people from all walks of life had risen, including

---

[2] This essay was written on the occasion of the 25th anniversary of the Tiananmen movement.

workers who quickly organized themselves into autonomous workers' associations. As a friend from Beijing Normal College (now Capital Normal University) told the author later that summer, "we were all there." It was the "city-people" (*shimin*) who bore the brunt of the government violence as they fought back to stop the troops from reaching the students in the square. The movement in Beijing triggered demonstrations in cities around the PRC, bringing out into the streets thousands of people of all walks of life, making the movement national.

To this day, it is not clear how many lost their lives—estimates range from the official hundreds to unofficial thousands. The numbers game is not likely to be resolved. The numbers are important so that the victims, named or nameless, may be preserved in historical memory, and the grief of parents and relatives assuaged. They are not crucial to assessing the criminality of the suppression. Even at the lower end, they stand witness to the hypocrisy of a state that would slaughter its own people in the name of defending them. The refusal to this day to acknowledge the crime is matched by continued criminalization of those who still live under the shadow of Tiananmen, and with courage continue to pursue the goals it had put on the political agenda—some from within the country, others from exile.

****

A *People's Daily* editorial published on 26 April 1989 that contributed significantly to the escalating confrontation between students and the authorities blamed the protests on an "extremely small number of people" whose "purpose was to sow dissension among the people, plunge the whole country into chaos and sabotage the political situation of stability and unity," and described the movement as "a planned conspiracy and a disturbance. Its essence is to once and for all, negate the leadership of the CPC and the socialist system." On June 5, in the immediate aftermath of the suppression, the State Council led by prime minister Li Peng issued an open letter addressed to the Party and the people that repeated some of the same charges and condemned the movement as a "counterrevolutionary riot" inspired by "Western" bourgeois ideas, instigated and financed by Hong Kong and overseas agitators. In the words of a *Beijing Review* editorial:

> The plotters and organizers of the counter-revolutionary rebellion are mainly a handful of people who have for a long time obstinately advocated bourgeois liberalization, opposed Party leadership and socialism and harbored political schemes, who have collaborated with hostile overseas forces and who have provided illegal organizations with the top-secrets of the Party and state…. Taking advantage of students' patriotic feelings…this handful of people with evil motives stirred up trouble.

There was a kernel of truth in the charge, calculated to confound a public whose hesitant exuberance had collapsed overnight into "no-exit" (*meiyou banfa*) pessimism. To quote from an article by this author written shortly after the event in collaboration with Roxann Prazniak:

> Chinese government charges of foreign involvement, while misguided in their suggestion of an organized conspiracy, are not vacuous…. There is hardly any question about the contributions of the

Voice of America which, as Chinese students proudly proclaim, shaped their understanding of the situation in the world, including the situation in China. Most intriguing is the conversion of the movement into a Chinese movement rather than a movement in the People's Republic of China. Chinese from Taiwan, the US and Hong Kong freely participated in the movement (in the PRC or from abroad) as if it were an ethnic movement and not a political movement in a sovereign state. Chinese secret societies were involved in smuggling people in and out of the PRC. And Chinese in Hong Kong freely admit (now with regrets) that funds from Hong Kong kept the movement alive past where it should have gone. It may be a function of racist attitudes toward the PRC (and Chinese) that the peculiarity of this situation, not to speak of its contribution to the final tragedy, has not been raised even as a question.

Nation-states thrive off the celebration of their glories. Just as avidly, they seek to bury in forgetfulness that which reflects badly on them, or to deflect blame onto others. The PRC is no exception but for the unswerving faith of the Communist Party leadership that the best way to deal with any blemish on its record is to prohibit public recognition and discussion, and then pretend it does not exist even when the said blemish is in full public view—as if the mask of infallibility were a guarantee of legitimacy and political survival. Charges against Tiananmen dissidents of conspiracy and collaboration with outside forces hostile to the national interest—also common items in the ideological tool-box nation-states draw upon to discredit dissent—were gross distortions of peaceful patriotic protests triggered by anxiety about economic distress, bureaucratic corruption, and intra-Party conflict that further deep-ened uncertainty over the future of the decade-long "reform and opening." But they served well to deflect attention away from the Communist Party, which increasingly had come to identify national with party interest—much like the warlords of an earlier day who had been targets of the revolution. "Counter-revolu-tionary riot" would become the official verdict on the movement. To this day, the Party has refused to budge from it—even with the rise to leadership of a genera-tion that in its youth had themselves been caught up in the ferment for reform and democracy.

* * * *

The PRC leadership has been quite successful in dimming memories of the event, and even turning it to political advantage, even though extinguishing memo-ries has proven to be more difficult than clearing the protestors from Tiananmen. The Party has been assid-uous in blacking out reference to Tiananmen in the media, including the internet. But it has not been able to silence the "Tiananmen mothers" who, like "*the Madres de Plaza de Mayo*" in Argentina or "*Cumartesi Anneleri*" (Saturday Mothers) in Turkey, have refused to give up on the struggle to force the state to account for their missing children. Occasional incidents of fatal punishment inflicted on jailed activists bring back into public consciousness those apprehended at the time languishing to this day in the anonymity of incarcera-tion. Others continue to call on the Party to reverse its verdict, knowing full well that they are likely to join their jailed comrades for their temerity. Most dramatic in these acts of remembrance are the annual demon-strations in Hong Kong to commemorate June 4, fueled by local anxieties about the progressive suffocation of freedom in the Special Administrative Region by oppressive practices emanating from Beijing, demographic "invasion" from the north that threatens everyday livelihood and welfare, and a corporate-dominated government that is more willing to follow Beijing's dictates than to share political power and responsibility with the people it governs. Modeled after the Tiananmen original in 1989, the Hong Kong "Goddess of Democracy" (*minzhu nushen*), "temporarily" housed at the Chinese University of Hong Kong, keeps alive memories of June 4 as inspiration for local autonomy and democracy.

Memories of Tiananmen are nevertheless challenged by increasing obliviousness to what the movement stood for, as well as to its present-day repercussions. The forgetfulness that comes with the passing of time is no doubt an important element. If time does not necessarily heal, it still throws over the past the cover of new concerns and challenges that filter the memories and give them new meanings. The "forgetting" in this case, is an enforced forgetting, which exacts pain and punishment for remembering, and denies to the generations who did not personally experience the event all knowledge of it except perhaps a passing reference now and then to the victory over the attempted counterrevolution by "an extremely small number" of misfits. Indeed, on a rare occasion when reference to Tiananmen has appeared in print, a newly acquired "soft power" approach has been in evidence in testimonials by experts on "how well China has done, economically and politically, since 1989, upholding the official verdict that the government acted correctly in crushing the 1989 protests." The experts variously attributed the incident to youthfulness, anxiety about the reforms, and an immature reliance on "the West" over native resources. If a Chinese millennial has any knowledge of the event, it is at best likely to be along the lines of the Harvard student who told her interlocutors that "the Chinese government is not evil. They did it out of good intentions. If they had had more appropriate equipment, they would have done a better job in 1989.... The Chinese government didn't tell the truth, but the West didn't tell the truth either because they didn't like China's rising." The knee-jerk patriotism of a foreign student in an alien environment is reinforced in the case of students from the PRC by an atavistic patriotic education intolerant of any criticism at home or abroad, whether the subject is Tiananmen, Tibet, Xinjiang or the Republic of China in Taiwan. That many of these students are offspring of Party cadres enriched by corruption adds an additional motivation for defense of the Party line.

Much more so than the passage of time or censorship, with the phenomenal economic, social and cultural transformation of the PRC during the past two decades, Tiananmen seems to belong to an entirely different age that is best left behind. This is the message conveyed by the apparent desire to shift emphasis from the event to the economic development made possible by political stability in its aftermath. It is likely the utmost desire of the Party itself. An eloquent example of this desire is the intriguing case of Wu'erkaixi, a student leader in the movement, who was among China's most wanted after June 4. Having managed to escape into exile, he studied in the US, and subsequently moved to Taiwan where he has been living for a number of years. In recent years, he has made a number of attempts to get himself arrested so that he can go back to see his aging parents. He has repeatedly been refused entry into the country. It is not every day that a country refuses to get its hands on its most wanted voluntarily submitted. It is difficult not to conclude that the Party simply does not want any of the publicity that would attend his return, especially a criminal trial guaranteed to open the gates to a flood of memories, and possibly serve as a lightning rod for social and political conflict. That Wu'erkaixi is of Xinjiang Uighur origin is no doubt an additional consideration of no little significance in the midst of ongoing government efforts to quell Uighur resistance to Han colonialism.

****

Government efforts to relegate Tiananmen to a different age have fallen on receptive ears both in the PRC and abroad. There is good reason for this because from both Chinese and global perspectives, it does belong in more than one sense in a different world than that of the present.

The suppression of the movement brought to an end a decade of uncertainty and unrest that had accompanied the changes ushered in by "reform and opening" after 1978. Tiananmen was a tragedy, not only because of what transpired the night of June 4, 1989, but also because it was the product of the seemingly inexorable sharpening of the contradictions in the course of the decade that the reforms had given rise to, culminating on the fateful events of that night. One of the most remarkable things about Chinese society in the 1980s was the contradictoriness of the messages it conveyed to the observer, within or without the PRC. Evidence of impressive economic progress on all fronts coexisted with accumulating evidence that something had gone very wrong. Continued economic growth was accompanied after 1985 with increasingly severe inflation (ranging from 30-50% annually), problems in agriculture (decline in grain production, shortage of fertilizer, and deterioration of the agrarian infrastructure), industry (failure to register increases in productivity). Increasing wealth for some was accompanied by problems of unemployment and poverty, exacerbating the problem of social division. Social vitality, evident in the flourishing of individual entrepreneurial activity, was accompanied by signs of social deterioration (appearance of beggary, prostitution and criminal activity ranging from petty theft and street muggings to organized crime in the peddling of drugs and sale of women and children) and social breakdown (ranging from worker strikes and peasant attacks on granaries to social banditry, including train robberies). Release of political controls to encourage economic growth was accompanied by unprecedented political corruption. The opening to the world which ushered in a cultural revival brought with it a cultural disorientation that not only intensified dissatisfaction with a seemingly incoherent socialist system beyond redemption but also produced disaffection with the very idea of being Chinese. The new emphasis on producing an educated elite was accompanied by decline in the educational system. New vitality in the realm of culture, unprecedented since the establishment of the People's Republic, was accompanied by alienation and moral indifference, even social irresponsibility. Students on campuses revolted against Party control which they felt obstructed the educational excellence that would be the guarantee of future prospects. The massive student demonstrations that erupted in December 1986 in east central China appear in hindsight as a dress rehearsal for what was to come in 1989. By late 1988 and early 1989, there was every sign that Chinese society was in deep trouble and that the reforms had run into a dead end. The government and the Communist Party, in turn, seemed incapable of dealing with the problems its policies had created, riddled as it was with corruption, factionalism and the organizational incoherence it displayed as these social and ideological tendencies worked their way into the very constitution of the existing political order.

The Tiananmen movement was the making of a generation that had come of political age in the midst of this social, cultural and political incoherence. Youth who had been rusticated during the Cultural Revolution were returning to the cities, radicalized by their experiences of poverty and backwardness in rural China that further had deepened their cynicism of the Communist Party. Their younger counterparts, born at the tail end of the Cultural Revolution, experienced politicization as they sought to overcome uncertainties provoked by the unsettled question of whether the future lay with socialism or capitalism. Party efforts to depoliticize them by the discipline of "socialist spiritual civilization" fell on deaf ears against evidence of Party corruption and infectious materialism. At the same time, criticism of the system by prominent intellectuals like Fang Lizhi and Liu Binyan reinforced a new political idealism nourished by exposure to novel political philosophies and cultural practices that came with the opening to the outside world. The mix of idealism and cynicism would be very much in evidence in 1989.

These contradictions disorganized the Party leadership even as they sought to bring the events under their control. The Party almost lost it in May–June 1989. The possibility acquired additional urgency from the global context. 1989 was to mark the end not just of historical socialism but the era of revolutions in modern history. Whether or not the PRC leadership in China perceived it in these historical terms is beside the point.

The Tiananmen movement was to prove every bit as profound in its consequences as the turn to reform ten years earlier. Between 1989 and 1992, when the decade-long enthusiasm for Deng Xiaoping of global capital turned into condemnations that made him into a villain second only to Mao Zedong, the Party leadership made a decision to resolve the contradictions that had brought about June 1989 simply by abolishing the entrapment between socialism and capitalism, opting for capitalism as the choice for China's immediate future. Deng's visit to the South in 1992, described in imperial terms (*nanxun*, or "progress to the South"), reaffirmed what had been accomplished in the special economic zone of Shenzhen. His conclusion that it was time not to worry about whether the path followed was socialist or capitalist, so long as it worked, echoed his statement of the early 1960s, that "it did not matter whether a cat was black or white so long as it caught mice." That had landed him in hot water for two decades as a "capitalist-roader." His injunction in 1992 had an electrifying effect, albeit in a politically antithetical direction, similar to Mao's statement back in late 1957 that "people's communes are good," which had led to the communalization of the country within months.

This time around, the message was to jump into the sea of capitalism, and many followed Deng's advice. The Party made a conscious decision at the time that consumption might well serve as a substitute for politics, so that there would be no repetition of Tiananmen in the future. The "spiritual solutions to material problems" of a decade earlier were now to be replaced by material solutions, at least for those sectors of the population prone to demands for political participation, whose political desire could be replaced by the desire for the good life. There was something of an important bargain here: so long as the Party delivered the goods, its leadership would go unchallenged. The freedom to consume would pave over the "cries for democracy." In the aftermath of Deng's trip to Shenzhen a local official quipped, "Let them [young people] have their desires! If they have money, they can do what they want. Just no more Tiananmens!" If hedonism was preferable to political involvement, Chinese capitalism of the kind associated with Singapore showed the way to controlling the socially degenerative consequences of capitalist development. In his talks in Shenzhen in 1992, Deng noted that through "strict management," Singapore had succeeded in preserving "social order" while developing rapidly. He thought that China could borrow from the Singapore experience to do even better.

The turn to a culture of consumption was accompanied from the early 1990s by a revival of "traditionalisms," symbolized by the term "Confucianism," that rounded out the circle by bringing together modernity and tradition, which had been an aspiration going back to the origins of the Chinese Revolution— except that it was neither the modernity nor the tradition that the revolution had sought to achieve. It was quickly obvious that Confucianism was subject to the same instrumentalization (and commodification) as socialism had come to be. The revival of tradition came as a relief to those who had mourned its passing all along. Official commentators were quite explicit that the revival of the Confucian tradition was intended to supply values of order and ideological unity at a time when the population had lost faith in socialism or its promises. Confucianism also held the promise of orderly development, as had been promoted since the early 1980s by cheerleaders of the authoritarian developmentalist regimes of Eastern Asia. The late 1980s had witnessed, side by side with the calls for democracy and "civil society," the promotion by some of so-called "new authoritarianism," inspired by right-wing political scientists in the United States such as Samuel Huntington. The Confucian revival was entangled in these various efforts to find remedies to the contradictions created by efforts to articulate socialism to capitalism. What most mattered in the end, however, was the offer of consumerism (of commodities, socialism, or Confucianism) in exchange for the abandonment of political democracy.

The bargain worked. And the circumstances were auspicious. The PRC's full-scale incorporation in global capitalism coincided with the globalization of capital with the fall of socialism globally. The PRC would emerge by the end of the decade as one of the motors of globalization. A labor force, trained by a socialist revolution carried out in its name, was now rendered into a forcefully submissive force of production for a global capitalism, in the name of a socialism that was postponed further and further into the future. Oppression and exploitation were still there, to be sure, but they could be pushed to the background as passing abnormalities soon to be replaced by plenty as the forces of production advanced, and the country had a genuine basis for socialism. In the meantime, consumer goods were made widely available to a population starved for them by decades of revolutionary puritanism.

Deng Xiaoping was the architect of these policies in a very real sense, but efforts to make him into a Chinese capitalist saint ignore his faithfulness to Bolshevik elitism, which was also his legacy to the reforms. His successor, Jiang Zemin, would complete the counter-revolution that Deng had initiated. By the early part of the twenty-first century, under Jiang's leadership, China was able to claim a place for itself among the ranking powers of the world—not by virtue of ideological priority as a socialist state but as a country on which capital globally had come to depend. It also had come to emulate other capitalist societies in the increasingly unequal distribution of wealth and welfare between classes, genders, and between urban-rural areas, as well as its contribution to pollution that threatened not just its own future but that of the globe as a whole. Jiang Zemin's "important thought of three represents," something of a joke even among Communist Party circles, sought to make the Party into an instrument of development that would serve the most "advanced" sectors of the country—which translated readily into the making of the Party into a party of the urban economic ruling classes. The contradictions this time around were not of socialism, but of successful incorporation in global capitalism.

The 1989 generation were products of a post-socialist milieu in which the experience of the Cultural Revolution was still very much alive despite its official repudiation in 1978, and the future of socialism still presented itself as a central issue of contention. The Communist Party has still not abandoned its pretensions to socialism, but its ritualized reaffirmations of "socialism with Chinese characteristics" have ceased to have any meaningful connection either to its own policies or to the population at large—except perhaps to legitimize the plunder of public goods in the name of development. In the two decades after Tiananmen, PR Chinese society has gone through further "cultural revolutions" that mock the Cultural Revolution Mao Zedong had launched to guarantee socialism as the PRC's future. In the late 1990s, the turn to markets, advertising and consumption were viewed by its agents some as a "second cultural revolution," more powerful by far than the original in its staying power. More recently, internet activism has been described as another "cultural revolution." Whatever we may choose to make of these appellations, they are indicative of the transformation of PRC society and culture.

Chinese millennials have come of age in the context of "China's rise" by successful exploitation of opportunities provided by the globalization of capital, which has also fueled nationalist fervor and cultural introspection. The restructuring of domestic spaces and the PRC's relationship to the world at large has induced the transformation of intellectual orientations and "the structures of feeling." Despite the cosmopolitization of everyday life that has accompanied the globalization of PRC society, however, in contrast to the Tiananmen rebels' thirst for cultural and philosophical understanding of the outside world, the present generation is shielded from the world outside by an education that instills in youth the provincial narrow-mindedness of an exuberant nationalism. The Tiananmen generation, too, had been raised on the nationalist education of the early 1980s that already sought in nationalism a substitute for socialism. But this was still a nationalism that drew its logic from a century of revolution. The nationalist ideology that came to the fore in the 1990s turned for inspiration to the very traditions that the revolution had sought to overturn. Even as the PRC inserted itself in global capitalism, it began to turn its back on the universalism that had informed the revolutionary movement. In this sense the PRC has followed a trajectory similar to that of the Guomindang in the 1930s. In its "superior" ability to police unwanted ideas of human rights and democracy, it has been more effective in enforcing among the people the provincial mentality of the Party itself.

The regime's efforts to depoliticize the population have worked, but only up to a point. Coercion is readily at hand to make up where ideological education falls short of silencing dissent. The PRC population readily expresses its frustrations on everyday matters. The agrarian population, popular source of the Chinese revolution, readily fights back against the state to protect its rights. The industrial sector is marked by frequent worker strikes against poor pay and oppressive working conditions. And though present-day concerns are different from the anxieties and hopes that drove the generation of 1989, youth is quite contentious. The contestation is there, but its effectiveness in achieving its goals should not be exaggerated. Party and government organs strictly regulate and circumscribe the sphere of protest, and are prepared to nip in the bud any tendency to politicize social issues.

It is not only Party control that conditions protest. It is constrained also by popular concerns about jeopardizing "China's rise." The Communist Party itself is by no means monolithic. It has its own advocates of greater democracy and the rule of law in governance. Popular ferment is also an eloquent indication of cravings for more effective civic and political participation and voice among social groups empowered by development. While talk about democracy (and kindred notions such as freedom and human rights) is an ongoing feature of political discourse within the Party and among the public at large, however, it would seem to be trumped for most people by concerns for stability and continued development.

These concerns are no doubt exacerbated by nationalist cravings for "China's rise." The patriotism instilled in youth by a chauvinistic nationalist education can even become an embarrassment in forcing the state to take positions in international relations it might well desire to avoid. Popular patriotism draws energy from its entanglement in pervasive aspiration to achieve the good life which may be fulfilled only by further "rise." In contrast to the anxieties of the earlier generation about the future—personal or national—the present generation is taught that the future belongs to the PRC—evidence for which seems to be readily available in the rapid advance of an otherwise obscene consumerism that has become a defining feature of present-day PRC culture, driven by a predatory global capitalism that looks to the PRC as the source of its future customers. Democracy is by all appearances a remote concern to the new "middle classes" so long as the Party can guarantee the freedom to consume.

It would be interesting, were it allowed, to see what the contentious internet clientele would make of the Tiananmen movement. Despite radical transformation, the two periods have commonalities arising from frustration with the despotic rule of the Communist Party. Party abuse of the people is an ongoing issue. So is the demand for democracy. The problem of inequality surpasses what the generation of 1989 might have dared to imagine. Private exploitation of public resources by Party members places the PRC among the most corrupt countries in the world. These commonalities might or might not enter the evaluation of June 4.

The views expressed by the Harvard student cited above are likely representative of prevailing sentiments, especially among the new generation. Such sentiments no doubt draw at least some plausibility from the subsequent careers of Tiananmen veterans who have gone their various ways, some of them to Wall Street, justifying suspicions that they had been motivated all along by elitism if not opportunism.

****

Memories of Tiananmen among the foreign public and scholars of China have also been significantly attenuated by the PRC's phenomenal development and the radical changes in its relationship to the world. The number two economic power in the world has quickly learned to emulate the imperial policies of number one, embellishing them with "Chinese characteristics" in which memories of the imperial tribute system of an earlier age are blended with the legacies of a revolution that for half a century sought to challenge the capitalist world order. Hype about "China's rise" celebrates the PRC's return to the "normalcy" of the capitalist world system. It is forgotten in the process that the PRC all along has been a major power, but as a Third World socialist threat to the global capitalist system. Those old enough may still remember US officials in the 1960s declaring solemnly that if the "Red Chinese" were not stopped in Vietnam, "we" would have to fight them in California!

The Tiananmen suppression brought back these memories of "Red China." The turn from revolution to reform in 1978 expectedly had been greeted with an orgy of enthusiasm for the PRC, and especially for Deng Xiaoping. For a decade, until the eve of the suppression, Deng was the golden-haired boy of Americans and Westerners in general. He was hailed as the greatest revolutionary of the twentieth century who had returned China to its proper historical path after three decades of aberrant revolutionary socialism. In the US, he had been named "man of the year" more than once (*Time*, 1979, 1985; *National Review*, 1985).

A decade of "China fever" evaporated when on June 4, 1989 the Communist Party called out the troops to put an end to the movement. In the aftermath, it was hard to find anyone to put in a good word for the Chinese government or its leaders, at least publically. The insults heaped upon Deng equaled in their negativity the extravagance of the praise bestowed upon him earlier. He was called a butcher, placed in a category reserved for the likes of Fidel Castro, Kim Il-sung, and the Romanian Communist dictator Nicolae Ceaușescu, and, perhaps most irredeemably, charged with resurrecting Mao Zedong's policies—a bugaboo of the US government, press, and many establishment China scholars. Scholars who had been admirers of his "revolutionary" policies discovered suddenly that those policies had created "the worst of all worlds." One professional anti-Communist, a consistent critic of the Communist Party, perceived in these uniformly negative appraisals "a remarkable and truly moving unanimity on the issue of China." Not everybody gave up on the PRC. Barely weeks after the suppression of the student movement President George Bush, Sr., sent in secret emissaries to deliver to Deng Xiaoping in person his letter hoping that the furor would soon die down and amicable relations re-established. Realist "soft anti-Communists" continued to hope that the PRC might yet be eased out of communism "peacefully" by the effects of a "market economy." Leaving aside ethical questions which are of little interest to "Realist" policy makers and advisers, they would be right in the long run—although from a contemporary perspective, the results are less than benign!

While suspicion of the PRC remained alive for the next few years, as relations with the outside world were "normalized," there was a return by the end of the 1990s to enthusiasm for the PRC which in the new millennium would reach orgiastic proportions, possibly unequalled since the European *Chinoiserie* craze of the seventeenth and eighteenth centuries. The China hype would reach a crescendo by the time of the 2008 Olympics and the 2010 Shanghai Exposition. It has been tempered somewhat since then in the face of the PRC's sneaky expansionist moves in Eastern and Southern Asia. But the PRC is still hot, if more of a threat to US hegemony and world peace, not to speak of the environmental health of the earth.

Underlying this China hype is the phenomenal economic development of the PRC that has catapulted it to second place in the world economy by GDP, even if on a per capita basis it remains one of the poorest countries in the world. The PRC, unsurprisingly, is an attractive example to many in the developing world who no doubt feel empathetic to its challenge to imperial Western domination of the last two-three centuries, and a counter-balance to a hegemonic US with a seeming addiction to war. More importantly, as it has emerged as the "factory of the world" and the primary consumer of developmental resources, it has created a "market dependency" that has made it indispensable to the continued welfare of economies around the world, including economies more advanced than its own. When the US and Europe were thrown into economic turmoil with the recession of

2008 their financial institutions had managed to engineer, the PRC's ability to overcome the adverse effects
of the recession made it into a beacon of salvation of
sorts for both businesses and populations in search of
a way out of their economic woes.

A most important aspect of these changes has
been the unprecedented expansion of social and
cultural exchanges. For the last decade, everyone—
from "wealth management" firms like Bain Capital, of
Mitt Romney fame, to all the major auto companies in
the world, from top-notch peddlers of luxury goods
from Europe to Hollywood, from US universities
opening up campuses in the PRC to National
Basketball Association players—has located in the
PRC as the new land of opportunity, with promises of
unbounded future riches of one kind or another. In
the capital in Beijing, the hyper-developed coastal
urban conglomerations around Guangzhou and
Shanghai, and Chongqing and Chengdu in the interior, expats share in the new life of luxury with few
equals in the world. There are more than 300,000
foreign students in the PRC. There are trading
communities of Africans, Arabs and others that are
reminiscent of trade in the treaty ports of imperial
China. So long as they stay out of politics—and the
sight of security—the PRC might seem to these
groups as an exciting playground, in many cases freer
than where they came from. They in turn are allowed
to bring world culture into the midst of Chinese society; at least so long as they stay away from those
aspects of world culture that might "hurt the feelings
of the Chinese people" or transgress "Chinese"
cultural and political norms—which include a great
many things from Tibet to Xinjiang, Falun gong,
Tiananmen, democracy, human rights, constitutional

government, etc., etc. Fair enough. If the Chinese people cannot speak about those things, why should foreigners?!

Movement in the opposite direction is equally intense. Going out into the world (*zouxiang shijie*— and now, *zouchuqu*, "getting out" pure and simple) has almost become obligatory for professors and government personnel. The Kennedy School at Harvard has become home away from home for top-level officials who receive instruction in the latest methods of political management (including "soft power"), followed by institutions like the Sanford School of Public Policy at Duke University for lower-ranking personnel. In cumulative numbers, two and a half million PRC students have been schooled abroad. The great majority of them have stayed abroad, peopling business, and cultural and educational institutions. Since 2004, approximately 500 Confucius Institutes have been established around the world (around 100 in the US) to add what officialdom considers to be "Chinese culture" to the PRC's many exports. The PRC has its own colonies in the Chinese laborers sent abroad to work on projects abroad, many of them government funded. We could add to these officially sanctioned exports the many—poor peasants to multi-millionaires—who move abroad in search of livelihood or to secure their wealth, some of it ill-begotten. If world culture has become part of the PRC, it is also the case that "Chinese culture" in one form or another has become part of global cultural sensibility.

These changes have also transformed the Communist Party. As Mao suits have given way to Western garb, Marxist literature has been replaced in the Party's education by management texts. In the Party and national institutions like the National

People's Congress, billionaires and millionaires have unseated the peasants and workers who had made the revolution against them. Remarkably, through these radical changes, the Party has stuck to the narrative of revolution, adding a new chapter to it with every change of leadership, construed as one more step in the unfolding of "socialism with Chinese characteristics." In 1989, the movement's suppression was justified by charges of "counter-revolutionary" conspiracy to overthrow socialism. For the last decade, renaissance and renewal have replaced revolution. The revolutionary narrative now incorporates elements from native traditions that a century of revolution had sought to overcome and eradicate. But the Party still presents itself as the personification of the revolution and the nation, and defender of "socialism with Chinese characteristics" against any attempt to turn the country in a liberal "bourgeois" direction. In foreign affairs, too, it invokes its "semi-colonial past" to manufacture a sense of kinship with people of the Global South. It disguises its expansionism with the cloak of anti-imperialist struggle to retrieve territories "stolen" from it by imperialists of a former age. And it continues to behave as if it is still determined to pursue the revolutionary goal of transforming the global order dominated by the same old imperialists. What this new order might be is puzzling to the outsider, as the PRC's economy is already integrated with that of the global capitalist economy, and its new ruling class (including top officials in the Party) hobnobs with the new transnational capitalist class. Unlike in Cold War days, the political and military supremacy the PRC seeks is hard to credit as anything but a striving for imperial hegemony within the global capitalist order. Nevertheless, legacies of the revolution are readily available to justify continued containment of political and cultural demands from its citizens, and to cloak imperial activity abroad.

None of this should be news to anyone even remotely connected with PRC affairs. Nevertheless, PRC leaders have been quite successful in containing foreign criticism as well through a combination of hard and soft power. While military threats to neighbors have become commonplace, economic blackmail still provides the most effective weapon against those who displease the PRC by thwarting its imperious (and imperial) claims. The PRC readily uses the threat of denying economic participation in its riches to retaliate against anyone who contradicts one or another of its proliferating claims (as in the case of its neighbors in eastern Asia, India and Australia), or breaks one of its prohibitions—especially regarding the Dalai Lama. Visiting dignitaries are regularly chastised for their transgressions. It denies visas to foreign journalists who in the authorities' opinion report unfavorably on its leadership. Scholars are denied visas for their work on the oppressed minorities, especially in Tibet and Xinjiang. When a US citizen of Taiwanese descent decided to have a mural on Tibet painted on a building he owned in the small town of Corvallis that is home to Oregon State University, officials from the PRC Consulate in San Francisco were dispatched to warn the mayor of consequences if the "transgression" was not stopped. Most recent are the unpleasant chauvinistic confrontations that surrounded President Obama's arrival in Hangzhou for the G-20 meeting.

The hubris of PRC officialdom has been puffed-up by the adulation extended to them by those filled with awe at the country's economic growth and promises, as well as by an Orientalist inflation of its cultural charms, which reached fever pitch between the Beijing Olympics of 2008 and the Shanghai Expo in 2010, both of which set new standards in vulgar excess. The PRC has deployed "soft power" tactics to exploit this adulation. The most egregious product of its efforts to project "soft power" has been the notorious "Confucius Institutes," already referred to above.

"Soft power" was proposed by the Harvard scholar Joseph Nye to refer to the intangible aspects of power (such as cultural power) that make its holders attractive, and enable persuasion rather than coercion in international relations—sort of like the Gramscian notion of hegemony. Propaganda may be part of it, but it is more than propaganda, at least in the sense of disguising or misleading. It also entails offering the self as an example that others may be tempted to emulate. The PRC deployment of the idea has reduced "soft power" to propaganda, which possibly also has something to do with the Chinese notion of propaganda (*xuanchuan*), that conveys also a sense of propagation, dissemination, making known, and, therefore, education. Be that as it may, "Confucius Institutes" are governed by an "autonomous" unit (Hanban) directly under the PRC Ministry of Education, but ultimately under the propaganda branch of the Party, as is the Ministry of Education itself, along with many other units of Party and government, including the Party's own research institutes. Remarkably, the PRC was successful in placing these institutes on university campuses where, in addition to teaching and cultural activity, they could also keep an eye on scholarly activities that went against its prohibitions, and if possible head them off—this is at least the impression yielded by a number of incidents around the world to keep the Dalai Lama or talk of Taiwan independence off campuses. The refusal—in violation of the equal opportunity laws of Canada—of the institutes to hire members of the Falun Gong, has recently led the Canadian Association of University Teachers to call for the dismissal of the institutes from college and university campuses. Spurious comparisons to the German Goethe Institutes or the Alliance Française ignore that these institutions are not located on university campuses, and are not subject to the kinds of restrictions that are demanded of the Confucius Institutes by the dictates of the propaganda bureau. Soft power in service of cultural attraction should include the living culture of society, not just its clichéd historical legacies. This is rather a challenge in the case of the PRC where some of the most creative intellectuals and artists who are admired globally find themselves in jail, under house arrest, or subject to severe restrictions on speech and creativity. Defenders of these institutes have been silent over the removal from Tiananmen of the statue of the sage after whom they are named. Intellectually oriented Party members scoff at the song-and-dance version of Chinese culture that the institutes promote, while linguists have complained of their restriction of Chinese language teaching to official mandarin, which is more and more problematic as local languages assert themselves in daily life in the PRC.

The primary acknowledged goal of the institutes is to spread the teaching of Chinese language and culture around the globe. One of their most remarkable characteristics, however, is to bring cultural and business relations together in the localities where they are established, while sugar-coating cultural work with the promise of economic benefits. This was a major attraction in many instances in the US, especially in the midst of the economic recession. As the institutes have spread, they have diversified, tailoring their offerings to their broader institutional contexts. While the Hanban has refrained from imposing restrictions on a university like Stanford which no doubt seems like a plum catch, where they can in lesser universities and smaller institutions they have not hesitated to assert their prerogatives. Their cultural offerings range from food to theater, dance and music, depending on what the local market offers or demands. It is interesting that university and college administrators, who are displeased with charges against them of the restriction of academic freedom, refuse to make public the agreements they have signed with the Hanban on the grounds that concealment was part of the agreement!

The receptivity extended to the Confucius Institutes is inexplicable given their insipid contribution to university education in a country like the US where studies of China have been a significant part of the academic curriculum for half a century, not to speak of top institutions like Stanford, Columbia or the University of Chicago. Scholars of China, of course, always want more China studies. University administrators always want money—especially when outside sources are dwindling, as has been the case in the US for some time. The culture-business-education nexus of the institutes has also arrived at an opportune time, when business seeks to shape education and educational institutions behave increasingly like businesses. The combined pressures of business interest and the ideology of globalization have shifted attention from the education of citizens to the training of global citizens—for whom the PRC may well be a destination as the seemingly top player in the global economy. Past concerns about "conflict of interest" between donors of funds (including the state) and academic freedom have retreated before financial interest and business pressure. Since the September 11 attacks on the New York World Trade Center, dissident academics have been punished for speaking out against US policies or Israel, raising questions about the realities of academic freedom in the US, let alone elsewhere. A reductive multi-culturalism demands that "the other" must be respected—no matter how despicable. The PRC's success at capitalism without democracy has made authoritarianism respectable in influential quarters who perceive the "exuberance of democracy" as an obstacle to efficient business and government. The behavior of the global elite in recent years has confirmed long-standing doubts that capital's commitment to democracy stops at the boundaries of the so-called "market economy." In the Orwellian language of a Trilateral Commission report in 1975,

> ...the effective operation of a democratic political system usually requires some measure of apathy and non-involvement on the part of some individuals and groups.... In itself, this marginality on the part of some groups is inherently undemocratic, but it has also been one of the factors which has enabled democracy to function effectively.

Ironically, the multi-culturalism that calls for cultural sensibility to others also views with disdain "cultural imperialist" advocacy of democracy, human rights, universal values, and so on and so forth, ignoring the importance of these to millions in the Global South, including in-between societies such as the PRC, India, Turkey and many others. It does not seem anything out of the ordinary under these circumstances to find US university professors who respond to criticisms of the mistreatment of their colleagues in

the PRC by questioning the appropriateness of apply-
ing the "Western" idea of academic freedom to other
societies.

It will be interesting to see, in this context, how
educational institutions will remember Tiananmen—if
they do at all. It is more than likely that they will view
it as a nuisance dragged out of the past. There are many,
of course, who are unhappy with the trends I have
observed above, including many scholars of the PRC
and Chinese intellectuals and academics working abroad
or in exile. Hong Kong will remember for sure, and the
tragedy will be the subject of much notice in academic
publications and the press. As far as US universities are
concerned, it remains to be seen. A group of concerned
scholars, intellectuals and concerned professionals have
circulated a letter to all the Confucius Institutes in the
US urging the commemoration of June 4. So far there
have been no takers!

* * * *

In historical perspective, the private and public trauma
of Tiananmen was also the trauma of the radical transformation of the PRC. It hardly matters whether
Tiananmen represented the death-pains of socialism
(by then, already post-socialism) or the birth-pains of
the authoritarian capitalist society that the PRC has
become. From a global perspective, it seems hardly
fortuitous that a decade-long unrest exploded in spring
1989. The very day of the suppression, the Solidarity
Union in Poland which had overthrown communism
there went to the polls for new elections. A few months
later the Berlin Wall fell. The rest, as they say, is history.

Less obvious but equally significant was the
context of "actually existing socialism" in the 1980s in

an ascendant neo-liberalism which would in short order be named "globalization." The transformation of societies globally over the last four decades has been marked by popular protest against forced subjection to the vagaries of a new global economy and the inequities it has created, devastating environmental deterioration that has accompanied the globalization of the developmentalist faith, and uncertainties about the future even among those who have been its beneficiaries. States have responded to proliferating popular protest by the intensification of authoritarian controls and repression that are very much the realities of contemporary life. Had the Tiananmen tragedy occurred today, it most likely would have been tagged as "Occupy Tiananmen" along with "Occupy Tahrir" or "Occupy Gezi." It had its antecedents, too, of which the most traumatic was the bloody overthrow in 1973 of the Allende government in Chile that in some ways inaugurated the neo-liberal era. This is easily overlooked in the US, as the overthrow of an elected communist government was "our" thing, unlike the Tiananmen suppression perpetrated by a Communist state. Henry Kissinger, the guiding light of "realists" in US foreign policy who has played a major part in "forgetting" Tiananmen infamously declared of the anti-Allende coup he had helped engineer in 1973 that "we cannot let a country go Communist due to the irresponsibility of its people." In a contemporary perspective, a proper commemoration of Tiananmen of necessity calls for deep reflection on our times, and what they may yet bring.

V

Mme. Xu's Excellent Adventure, or, What the PRC Wants

A scandalous incident took place at the recent twentieth biennial meeting of the European Association of Chinese Studies (EACS) in July 2014. The meeting, hosted by the venerable universities of Minho and Coimbra in Portugal, was devoted to the exploration of the development of China studies, entitled, "From the origins of Sinology to current interdisciplinary research approaches: Bridging the past and future of Chinese Studies." When they received their conference programs, the participants discovered that two pages had been torn out of the programs by the organizers, apparently at the insistence of Mme. Xu Lin, Director-General of the Hanban, in charge of the so-called Confucius Institutes, who in 2009 was appointed counselor to the State Council (the cabinet) with vice-ministerial rank, presumably in recognition of her contribution to the propaganda goals of the state. The pages torn out related to the Chiang

Ching-kuo Foundation in Taiwan, which long had sponsored the EACS and, according to a report in a Taiwanese newspaper, donated 650,000 Taiwanese yuan (around US$ 22,000) to that year's meeting. EACS investigation of the incident also found that, according to Mme. Xu, some of the abstracts in the program "were contrary to Chinese regulations, and issued a mandatory request that mention of the support of the CCSP [Confucius China Studies Program] be removed from the Conference Abstracts. She was also annoyed at what she considered to be the limited extent of the Confucius Institute publicity and disliked the CCKF [Chiang Ching-kuo Foundation] self-presentation."

This act of academic vandalism has been met with dismay, at least among those still capable of being shocked at the intrusion of PRC propaganda organs into the very institutional structures of academic work. If I may share here several responses from distinguished colleagues who must remain nameless since I do not have their permission to cite them by name:

A Danish historian who long has been involved with EACS:

> Indeed, what did the organizers of the conference and the EACS have in mind when accepting such a move? It is a very hot summer in Europe, but surely no excuse for not fighting Hanban considering the very long relationship between the EACS and the CCK Foundation. As far as I have understood the CCK Foundation did not even have any representatives present at the conference! Well, it is difficult in Europe in general fighting back Hanban's Confucius Institutes....

A distinguished historian of religion in China from the University of Paris, presently teaching in Hong Kong:

> Europeans are even more gutless than Americans, and clearly no less stupid. You are right: disgusting! Every book I put out in Shanghai I have to fight to get "CCK-financed" in the English acknowledgements. Impossible to put it in the Chinese version.

A US historian of religion commenting on a news item on the conference I had posted on Facebook:

> Moments like these when the veil drops are precious, let's hope it exposes some truths.

A distinguished anthropologist from Beijing University:

> the kind of "original rudeness" has been practiced for decades as "civility." A disgrace, urgently needing treatment.

And after I asked him to further explain these terms:

> by "civility" I usually refer to civilization; "original rudeness" is what I invent in English to describe the rough manners encouraged in Mao's time and continued to be performed until now. In old and new Chinese movies, we often see those boys or girls who look really straightforward and "foolish" are more attractive to their opposite sex. To some extent, the kind of rudeness has been seen as what expresses honesty... but the bad performance from the official of Hanban might just be another thing. I would see it as stupid; but other Chinese may see

it differently—some may be even proud of him [sic]. We can see from this that cosmopolitan civility is still needed in China.

I share these messages here to convey a sense of the deep frustration among many scholars of China with their impotence against the insinuation of PRC state and propaganda organs in educational institutions in Europe and North America. In the case of the colleague from Beijing University, there is also embarrassment at the delinquent behavior of a government official, combined with a different kind of frustration: that the act is unlikely to make much impression on a PRC academic and popular culture that is inured to vandalism if it does not actually condone it, beginning with the Party-state itself.

The frustration is not restricted to scholars of China. The Canadian Association of Higher Education Teachers and the American Association of University Professors have both rebuked universities in the two countries for allowing Confucius Institutes into universities and/or for their compliance with the terms set by the PRC. Faculties widely have been critical of the Institutes and, in response to criticism, a number of institutions in North America and Europe have terminated their association with the Hanban. The most thorough and eloquent criticisms of the institutes have been penned not by a China specialist but the distinguished anthropologist Marshall Sahlins. This broad involvement of university faculty indicates that the issues at hand go beyond Confucius Institutes or the PRC, and is revealing of accumulating frustration with significant trends that promise to end higher education as we have known it. The Institutes have been beneficiaries but also possibly the most offensive instance to date of the increasingly blatant administrative usurpation of faculty prerogatives in university governance, progressive subjection of education to business interests, and the normalization of censorship in education. At the behest of the Hanban for confidentiality, agreements over the institutes have been entered in most cases without consultation with the faculty, or at best with select faculty who, whatever the specific motivations may be in individual cases, display few qualms about complying with trends to administrative opacity or the secrecy demanded by the propaganda arm of a foreign state. The promise of the institutes to serve as bridges to business opportunities with the PRC has served as a major enticement, giving business and even local communities a stake in their acceptance and promotion, but further compromising academic autonomy. Despite all manner of self-serving protestations by those involved in the institutes, formally entered agreement to avoid issues that might conflict with so-called Chinese cultural and political norms—or whatever might "hurt the feelings of the Chinese people"—translates in practice to tacit self-censorship on questions the PRC would like to keep out of public hearing—the well-known issues of Taiwan, Tibet, June 4th, jailed dissidents, etc., etc. It also legitimizes censorship.

These issues concern, or should concern, everyone who has a stake in higher education. The questions facing scholars of China are narrower in focus and more specific to disciplinary concerns, but they may be even more fundamental and far-reaching in their implications than the institutional operations of the university. Beneath mundane issues of language teaching, teacher quality, and academic rigorousness lies a very important question: who controls the production of knowledge about China? Like other similar organizations, including the Chiang Ching-kuo Foundation, the Hanban has already entered the business of sponsoring research and conferences in research universities. But control is another matter. Interestingly, in its very vulgarity, Xu Lin's attempt to suppress the mention of a Taiwan competitor at an academic conference brings up this question more insistently than the sugar-coated representations of Confucius Institutes as simple providers of knowledge of Chinese language and culture to schoolchildren, or facilitators of business. The conjoining of teaching and business in Hanban activity itself should give us pause about easy acceptance of those representations. But the problem goes deeper.

It is a puzzle that a great many commentators in the US and Europe should be in self-denial about PRC aspirations to global hegemony when within the PRC it is a matter of ongoing conversation among Party leaders and influential opinion-makers, as well as the general public. To be sure, there is no end of speculation over elusive questions of whether or not and when the PRC might achieve global hegemony. But there is far less attention to the more immediate question of aspirations to hegemony—except among some on the right—possibly because it might fuel animosity and ill-feeling. It seems safer to go along with the more diplomatically innocuous official statements that all the PRC wants is equality and equal recognition, not world hegemony, even as it carves out spaces of "influence" around the globe.

In recent years, PRC leaders have made no secret that they wish to replace the existing world order over which the US presides. At the most modest level, President Xi Jinping's suggestion to the US President that the Pacific was big enough for the two countries to share as part of a "new great power relationship" was remarkable for its erasure of everyone else who lives within or around the Pacific. It would take the utter blindness of servile partisanship to portray PRC activity in eastern Asia, based on spurious historical claims, as anything but moves to establish regional hegemony which, John Mearsheimer has argued, is the first step in the establishment of global hegemony—a Monroe Doctrine for Eastern Asia. At the popular level, an obscure philosopher at the Chinese Academy of Sciences, Zhao Tingyang, has achieved fame nationally and in international power circles for his design of an alternative to the current international system based on a modernized version of the hierarchical "Under-Heaven" (*tianxia*) tributary system that informed imperial China until the early twentieth century.

Zhao's work is interesting because it has been acclaimed as a plausible example of the call for "IR theory with Chinese characteristics" that corresponds to the PRC's rising status—a call that eloquently brings together knowledge-production and the search for hegemony. The prevalent obsession with tagging the phrase "Chinese characteristics" onto everything from the most mundane to the most abstractly theoretical is well-known. But it seems to have acquired some urgency with the Xi Jinping leadership's apparent desire to regulate "Western" influence on scholarship and intellectual activity in general as part of his vaunted "China Dream" that also includes the elimination of corruption along with rival centers of power, enhancing Party prestige and control over society, and the projection of PRC hard and soft power both upon the global scene.

The policy blueprint laid down in the landmark third plenary session of the Eighteenth Central

Committee stressed "the strengthening of propaganda powers and the establishment of a Chinese system of discourse (*Zhongguo huayu xitong*) to propel Chinese culture into the world at large (*tuidong Zhonghua wenhua zouxiang shijie*)." The discourse is to be constructed upon the three pillars of "the fine tradition of making Marxism Chinese," or "socialism with Chinese characteristics," the creation of a contemporary Chinese culture by melding the Chinese and the foreign, and the old and the new. The Xi leadership's stress on the "ninety-year" revolutionary tradition—perhaps *the* foundation of Party legitimacy—is not necessarily in conflict with the plans for greater integration with the global neoliberal economy, since in Party theorization of "Chinese Marxism" the content of "socialism with Chinese characteristics" is subject to change in response to changing circumstances—and in accordance with the policies of each new generation of leaders. While the "China dream" is the subject of ongoing discussion, Xi Jinping has made his own the long standing "dream" of the rejuvenation and renaissance of the Chinese nation as the marker of "socialism with Chinese characteristics" under his leadership. Lest this be taken to be a return to a parochial conservatism, it is important to note that discussions of "Chinese discourse" note his emphasis on "making our own the good things from others" as well as "making the old serve the present" as fundamental characteristic of "Chinese" cultural identity. It might be recalled that the latter slogan caused much distress among foreign observers during the Cultural Revolution amidst reports that peasants, taking the slogan at its word, had begun to dismantle the Great Wall to use its stones to build homes for themselves! Presently, according to President Xi, the rich products of this 5000-year-old tradition should be taken out to the world to foster awareness of the universal value of a living Chinese culture that transcends spatial and temporal boundaries in its rich intellectual and artistic achievements. He also called upon Chinese scholars around the world to "tell China's story" (*Zhongguode gushi*). He himself is the most-travelled Chinese supreme leader ever, practically assuming the role of salesman for PRC policies and business.

A PRC expert on foreign relations and the US active in global international relations or circles has provided a convenient summary of Party leaders and intellectuals' close attention to "discursive struggles" over the last decade, beginning with the Hu Jintao leadership, and its institutional and intellectuals issues. The motivation, as he puts it, was to carve out a political cultural space of its own corresponding to the PRC's rising stature as a world power: "Although China has already joined the mainstream international community through this policy [Deng Xiaoping's opening-up policy], one of the main findings of the paper is that China does not want to be a member of the Western system. Instead, China is in the process of developing a unique type of nation-building to promote the Chinese model in the coming years." The formulation of a Chinese discourse was both defensive and promotional: to defend the PRC against its portrayals as a threat to world economy and politics, but at the same time to promote an image that would enhance its reputation in the world as a counterpart to a declining US hegemony caught up in constant warfare, economic problems, cultural disintegration and waning prestige.

It is interesting, however, that revamping the propaganda apparatus in public relations guise drew its inspiration mainly from the US example. The major inspiration was the idea of "soft power" formulated by Joseph Nye. US public relations practices and institutions are visible in everything from sending intellectuals out to the world to present a picture of PRC realities as the "Chinese people" perceive them to hosting international events, from publication activity in foreign languages to TV programming, from students sent abroad to students attracted to the PRC, and in the wholesale transformation of the very appearance and style of those who presented the PRC to the world. The idea of discourse was of Foucauldian inspiration, subject to much interpretation and misinterpretation. But its basic sense was quite clear. Participants in the discussion of discursive power and in its institutional formulations "all emphasize discourse as a kind of power structure and analyze the power of discourse through the lens of dominant characteristics such as culture, ideology and other norms. They consist of the ways we think and talk about a subject matter, influencing and reflecting the ways we act in relation to it. This is the basic premise of discourse theory." And they all share a common goal. In the author's own words, without editing:

> Obviously, China chooses to join the international society led by a western value held concept from thirty years ago, but it did not plan to accept completely the named "universal value concept" of the western countries, nor wish to be a member of those countries. Instead, China wishes to start from its national identity and form a world from China's word, and insist in the development road with Chinese characteristics, so as to realize the great revival of the Chinese nation. In order to realize this century dream, China is busy drawing on its discursive power and achieving this strategy with great efforts in public diplomacy.

Confucius Institutes (going back to 2004) were conceived as part of this discursive struggle, with "Confucius identified as a teaching brand to promote the [sic] Chinese culture." Language teaching was crucial to this task. The number of foreigners learning Chinese ("40 million" at last count although it may be much higher since the institutes progressed in numbers) is itself a matter of pride, but the ultimate goal is the assimilation of "Chinese culture" through introduction to the language and whatever cultural resources may be available locally (from art, opera, singing and dancing to cooking and wine tasting). It would be good to know how so-called Chinese culture is actually represented in the classroom beyond these consumer routines. Available ethnographies of the Institutes that I am aware of fall short, partly because of the opaqueness (at the "mandatory request" of Hanban) of their operations and partly because of a proclivity on the part of interlocutors with postcolonial sensibilities to privilege local agency over constraints imposed on performance by less visible and seemingly remote structures of power. Mme. Xu was quite (inadvertently) explicit in a recent BBC interview about the requirements imposed upon Institute teachers, including reports on activities concerning the PRC in their home universities.

One of the most interesting and probably far-reaching aspect of Hanban educational activities is to employ higher education Confucius Institutes as platforms to reach out into the community and public school classrooms. While we may only guess at the intentions behind this outreach, I think it is plausible to assume that they are not there to train future China specialists, although that, too, may happen, but to create cultural conditions where "China" ceases to be foreign, and acquires the same kind of familiarity that most people around the world have with United States cultural activity and products; at its best, to feel at home in a Chinese world. Kids in kindergarten and elementary school are more likely to be amenable to this goal than the less reliable college students!

Lest it seem that I am reading too much into this activity, let me recall a portrayal of an imaginary ("dreamlike?") Chinese world by Tu Wei-ming, former Harvard professor, prominent promoter of Confucianism as a global idea, and presently founding Dean of the Institute for Advanced Humanistic Studies at Beijing University—a highly respected and influential senior intellectual. In an essay published in 1991, he offered the following as a description of what he called "cultural China":

> Cultural China can be examined in terms of a continuous interaction of three symbolic universes. The first consists of mainland China, Taiwan, Hong Kong, and Singapore—that is, the societies populated predominantly by cultural and ethnic Chinese. The second consist of Chinese communities throughout the world, including a politically significant minority in Malaysia...and a numerically negligible minority in the United States.... The third symbolic universe consists of individual men and women, such as scholars, teachers, journalists, industrialists, traders, entrepreneurs, and writers, who try to understand China intellectually and bring their conceptions of China to their own linguistic communities. For the last four decades the international discourse on cultural China has been shaped more by the third symbolic universe than by the first two combined...Sinologists in North America, Japan, Europe, and increasingly Australia have similarly exercised a great deal of power in determining the scholarly agenda for cultural China as a whole.

"China's rise" over the last two decades has reconfig-ured the geography of "cultural China," and the dynamics of the interaction between these three "symbolic universes," with the relocation of the "center" in mainland China which now seeks to bring the other two spheres under its hegemony. We need not view Tu's description as some kind of blueprint in order to appreciate the valuable insight it offers into reading the contemporary situation. The PRC seeks to bring under its direct rule the Chinese societies of Hong Kong and Taiwan, with Singapore somewhat more problematic given its distance from the mainland, and this despite the fact that it served as a model for PRC development beginning in the 1990s. Chinese overseas are obviously a major target of PRC cultural activity, especially now that their numbers are being swelled by new immigrants from the PRC with consid-erable financial and political clout; in the run-up to the Toronto School Board decision on whether or not to allow Confucius Institutes (they decided not to) in October 2014, the PRC Consul General Fang Li was able to successfully mobilize the Hua population in support of the Institutes. What I have discussed above—and the Xu Lin episode—provide sufficient evidence, I think, to indicate the significance placed upon expanding the third sphere, and shaping its activ-ities. Hegemony over the production of knowledge on China is crucial to this end.

There is nothing particularly earth-shattering about this activity except that the PRC's habitual conspiratorial behavior makes it seem so. We may observe that the PRC is doing what other hegemonic powers—especially the US—have done before it: recruit foreign constituencies in the expansion of cultural power. To put it in mundane terms, as the so-called "West" established its global hegemony by creating "westernized" foreigners, the PRC in search of hegemony seeks through various means to expand the sphere of "Chinized" foreigners, to use the term offered by the author of the article discussed above.

There has been considerable success over the last decade in promoting a positive image for the PRC globally, although it is still unclear how much of this success is due not to cultural activity but the economic lure of a fast developing economy. PRC analysts are quite correct to feel that this may be the opportune moment, given that the existing hegemon is mired in social division, dysfunctional political conflict, continual warfare and a seeming addiction to a culture of violence. It is also the case that the craze for what is called "development" trumps in the eyes of political leaders and large populations around the world qualms about human rights and democracy, especially where these are not major concerns to begin with.

It is also the case that similarly to its predecessors going back to the Guomindang in the 1930s, the current PRC regime has been unable to overcome a nativist provincialism intertwined with anxieties about the future of the Communist Party that is a major obstacle to its hegemonic aspirations. Complaints about cultural victimization and national humiliation sit uneasily with assertions of cultural superiority and aspirations to global hegemony. Hankerings for a global *tianxia* ignore that despite the scramble to partake of the PRC's economic development, other nation-states are just as keen about their political sovereignty and cultural legacies as the PRC itself—just as surely as they are aware of the spuriousness of claims to genetic peacefulness when PRC leaders, with enthusiastic support from public opinion, openly declare that "national rejuvenation" includes the recapture, if necessary by violence, the domains of their imperial predecessors, and then some. Pursuit of the globalization of so-called "Chinese culture" is accompanied by a cultural defensiveness that tags "Chinese characteristics" to everything from the most mundane everyday practices to crucial realms of state ideology. Claims of universal value for Chinese cultural products are rendered questionable by the simultaneous denial of universality as a tool of "Western" hegemony. PRC leaders and their spokespeople officially deny any aspirations to global hegemony, needless to say, but then we might wonder what they have in mind when they accuse other powers of "obstructing China's rise," when those powers celebrate the PRC's economic development on which they have become dependent, and allow its propaganda organs into their educational systems! Similarly, if the goal is not hegemony over knowledge production about "China," why would these same leaders and their functionaries be so concerned to show the world the universal value of Chinese civilization, when that is already very much part of the global perception that has made the PRC the beneficiary of a benign Orientalism—or tear out pages of a conference program on the Chiang Ching-kuo Foundation which shares the same goal of promoting "Chinese" civilization?

While the new "public relations" approach has yielded impressive results, discursive struggle entails more than a competition in the global cultural or "discourse market," but finds expression also in the suppression of competing discourses at home and abroad. The "good things" from the outside world do not include the seven deadly sins which have been expressly forbidden as "dangerous western influences":

universal values, freedom of speech, civil society, civil rights, the historical errors of the Chinese Communist Party, crony capitalism, and judicial independence. While the PRC boasts a constitution, talk of matters such as "constitutional democracy" is not to be permitted. A prohibition against the use of terms like "democracy," "dictatorship," "class," etc., has been in effect for some time and, according to a colleague from Shanghai, authorities look askance at the use even of a seemingly word like "youth" (qingnian) in titles of scholarly works. Just recently, the Institute of Modern History of the Chinese Academy of Social Sciences was chosen by the Party Central Commission for Discipline Inspection as the location from which to warn the Academy that "it had been infiltrated by foreign forces." More recently, control over CASS has been expanded to include the ideological vetting of academic dissertations. An editorial on the internet, published in the *People's Liberation Army Daily* in mid-May 2015, upped the attack by referring to "traitors":

> If we don't occupy the internet, someone else will. If we don't defend this territory, we will forfeit it, which could even allow hostile forces to use it to attack our bridgehead.... Hostile Western forces and a minority of ideological traitors within the country are using the internet to attack our Party, discredit China's leaders, vilify our heroes.... The goal is to use the concept of "universal values" to confuse us, to use "constitutional democracy" to bring us disorder, to use color revolutions to topple us, to use negative public opinion to overturn us.

The persecution and incarceration of both Han and Minority scholars and activists who transgress against these prohibitions is a matter of daily record.

The same commentator who was cited above for the reference to a "global discourse market," writes that "basically speaking," the prohibitions have not changed the widespread attitude of reverence in the intellectual world for things western, "the blind and superstitious following of western scholarship and theories, and entrapment in the western 'discourse pitfall' (*xianjin*)." People may contend all they want, she concludes, but the discourse we need is one with Chinese "airs" (*fengge*) that strengthens China's "discursive power"(*huayu quan*). This translates in practice to the construction of theories (including Marxism) and historical narratives built around Chinese development (with the Party at its core) that may also serve as inspiration if not an actual model for others.

Interestingly, the "Western" ideas that the PRC regime deems inimical to its cultural security served the Communist Party well for three decades when demands for "democracy" and social justice and equality were inscribed on revolutionary banners. And it is conveniently ignored that in most discussions of "socialism with Chinese characteristics" that Marxism happens to be a "Western" idea, very much entangled in questions of democracy.

US business—and political—leaders seem to share an infinite faith that capitalism and democracy go hand in hand. Disney, Hollywood, automotive companies, and consumption of luxury goods by a growing PRC consuming class are in this view far more effective vehicles of universal norms than abstract talk about oppression and human rights. They may be right in some limited sense, but the PRC's rise, no less than the contemporary challenges to democracy of economic inequality and social incoherence in advanced capitalist societies, calls into question easy assumptions about a necessary causal relationship between capitalism and democracy. PRC leaders insist, of course, that despite immersion in global capitalism, theirs is a socialist market economy—which, judging by its structural strains, is also open to question in a long-term perspective. The future, if there is one, lies in the shadows.

Be that as it may, they give little indication of fears that democracy might follow in the wake of Mickey Mouse and Lamborghinis, which not only have escaped inclusion among the "bad things from the West" but find ready welcome among the new capitalist elite. Indeed, the PRC has lent further credibility to a harsher and lawless form of corporate "authoritarian capitalism" exemplified since the 1980s with Eastern Asian development, especially Singapore under Lee Kwan Yu who served as an inspiration for PRC policies beginning in the early 1990s.

Most interesting—and disheartening—is the response to the suppression of "academic freedom" of US scholars who would rather have the Confucius Institutes than defend "academic freedom," which they perceive as a "Western" thing that should not be imposed on others (and perhaps even on ourselves!). The irony is that many scholars in the PRC—and around the world—crave this "Western" thing, which is hardly just "Western" anymore, regardless of its origins. Respected scholars I am familiar with, some of them Party members, even think the Confucius Institutes are silly misrepresentations of "Chinese culture." They are also happy not to be in Saudi Arabia. It makes one wonder: which side are we on?!

VI
The Rise of China— and the End of the World as We Know It

The evidence is all around us, and yet it is still not easy to overcome a sense of the absurd prognosticating of the end of the world. Authoritative analysts of capitalist modernity like Fredric Jameson and Slavoj Žižek tell us that "it has become easier to imagine the end of the world than to imagine the end of capitalism." According to sociologists and social analysts such as John Bellamy Foster and Naomi Klein, certain doom awaits us anyway if we cannot imagine the end of capitalism. What they have to say carries a great deal of empirical weight, backed by ethical and social commitments. Unbridled capitalism has created an ecological and social crisis that is readily recognized by all but the most intransigent of its perpetrators. In its ethical dimension, contemporary capitalism fosters a culture of self-indulgent consumerism and a developmentalist mentality that refuses to give up on faith in the limitless exploitability of nature, and the equally limitless powers of technology to overcome any obstacles an embattled nature might throw up. Contemplating the end of the world might serve as an antidote to a faith that increasingly seems illusory. Still, it is no easy task to imagine the end of the world—except for the religious zealot or like-minded secular counterparts suffering from incurable addiction to apocalyptic thinking.

I may or may not be one of the latter, but accumulating evidence seems overwhelming. Difficult as it is, there is much to be gained from imagining the end of world in thinking through some of the more intractable problems of the present. The end of the world as we know it may be understood in two senses. The end of the world in a literal sense, which is no longer the purview of a lunatic fringe or religious millenarianism but has moved to the center of global concerns, backed with the authority of science, so that it is those who would deny the possibility that appear as the unredeemable lunatics. Less drastically but equally poignantly, it suggests the end of the world as we have known it, which is a fate that has befallen many with the rise of the modern world, who now seek to recover what they have lost, threatening to bring the same fate upon the victors of modernity.

The PRC figures prominently in both senses. Under the sign of a "new hegemony," the PRC has engaged in an expansionist policy in its immediate region pursuant to, it has been suggested, a grab for global power, with dreaded consequences in global conflagration. Changing the global order has been a long-standing goal of the Chinese revolution. The revolution may lie in ruins, but that goal persists. Despite success within the parameters of global capitalism, PRC leaders and their IR advisers repeatedly have expressed a desire to be its nemesis, not merely to reconfigure power relations within those parameters but to replace the Westphalian system of international relations by something akin to the so-called *tianxia* tributary system that prevailed in late imperial China. Nor is it just the international system. Here, too, we are all familiar with the ongoing suppression within the PRC of discourses of human rights, democracy, freedom, constitutional government, etc., that are considered to be "Western" viruses, to be purged by the rejuvenation of an imperial Confucianism. The PRC's economic success has given a new respectability to a neo-traditional authoritarianism. If the literal end of the world may somehow be averted, there is still little question that PRC leaders' vision of the world is very much at odds with the world as he have known it for some time.

The ecological consequences of the PRC's "rise" have given further substance to fears of the end of the world in its second, more apocalyptic sense: the literal end of the world as rapid environmental degradation and increasing pressure on resources push the earth beyond its capacity to sustain human life. To underline the negative aspects of the PRC's development is not to denigrate its achievements, or to suggest that it is responsible single-handedly for the threat to the sustainability of human life. But it may hardly be ignored that the development has come at great cost to the environment and even large numbers in the population. The wealth and power development has brought continues to lure the outside world. It also raises questions about what "development" means when it pulls the rug out from under its own feet. This question is once again receiving attention with the deep problems that have appeared in the PRC economy, turning fickle world spectators from great expectations to accumulating doubts. Predictions of China rise/China fall, China survive/China collapse, China will rule the world/China will not rule the world have become a favorite sport not only of daily reporting but academic specialists and pundits. They may not tell us much about the future but they are unmistakable evidence of persistent ambivalence.

The ecological crisis touched off by the PRC's development needs little by way of demonstration or elaboration, as daily headlines bring to the world's attention one manifestation after another of the cata-strophic environmental consequences of three decades of reckless maldevelopment. As I compose these lines (on October 7, 2015), the news is about tennis players choking and getting sick in a world-class tournament in Beijing, and a "carpocalypse," a fifty-lane traffic jam on an expressway to the capital one paper captions as "highway to hell." A recent report from University of California, Berkeley researchers found that recent years have witnessed the death of one and a half million people per annum due to pollution related causes. Air and water pollution, along with unsafe food, are among the top concerns of the population. Successive leaders have acknowledged the crisis as an impediment to further development and a threat to public welfare, the PRC is a global leader in clean energy, and President Xi recently has announced measures to control pollution. The economic recession has possibly provided some relief. But the devastation goes on.

Headlines are intended to lure the reader. Even so, these headlines, and the testimonials given in the reports, offer good cause to wonder if the PRC's devel-opment does indeed signal the end of the world as we have known it. Not just the "the demise of the capital-ist world economy," as world-systems analyst Minqi Li has suggested, but the world as earth, a livable habitat for its denizens. So rapid has been the PRC's rise to a world economy, so voracious its consumption of resources, and so far-reaching the environmental destruction by development that it invokes metaphors of apocalypse—as with the chronic "airpocalypses" in North China. We have become inured to photographs of coal waste by thousands of tons billowing out of dark towering chimneys, automobiles barely creeping along highways jammed as far as the eye can see, ghostly shadows of people shrouded in dark gray smog in seemingly futile search of their destinations, rivers turned into all colors of the rainbow by spilled chemicals, porcine carcasses by the thousands floating past glittering sky-scrapers.... The sights they capture match the darkest imaginings of cinematic apocalypse. In the recent airpocalypse episode in December 2015, it was reported that two Canadian entrepreneurs marketed cans of Rocky Mountain air which proved to be in great demand!

The pollution is not merely domestic either. Meteorologists have detected mercury from emissions in Chinese coal plants on Mt. Bachelor in Oregon, purportedly the cleanest place in the US until recently. The US Northwest is under pressure from mining interests in Montana and Wyoming to construct ocean terminals for shipping coal to "Asia." It is likely that the PRC would be an intended destination for oil flowing from Alberta to Houston if the promoters of the Keystone pipeline had their way. From Southeast Asia and Australia to Latin America but especially Africa, the PRC has added its considerable weight to the environmental destruction perpetrated by global mining and oil companies. PRC dams in Tibet threaten not only the local ecology but the ecology of South Asia from

India to Vietnam. Southeast Asian forests are under assault by the demand for wood products. From Nicaragua to Brazil, PRC transportation projects have met with widespread local and indigenous resistance for their obliviousness to the environment and local livelihood. The "rise" lives up to all the anxieties of eco-minded critics of unbridled development about the future of the earth as habitable environment. It should cause even greater trepidation that "China's rise" has inspired others from India to Africa and Latin America. Daily news from India, already no paragon of environmental health and a match for the PRC in damage to the environment, is replete with enthusiastic predictions that India is about to overtake the PRC in its rate of growth. In his shocking account of environmental and social devastation in Tibet, the Vancouver writer Michael Buckley suggests that Party leaders suffer from a "tunnel vision" in their faith that the answer to problems created by development is more development. The "tunnel vision" is not just theirs!

It would be self-serving if not an excuse for the perpetuation of colonial privileges for those in advanced capitalist societies to blame intensifying environmental crisis on the PRC or other developing societies, when it is these same "advanced" societies that forced others onto the path of development they had carved out at the threat of extinction. Nor may we overlook their complicity in the social and environmental consequences of the PRC's development as direct participants in production and indirect beneficiaries in consumption. On the very day in January 2013 when Beijing was choking under smog visible from space, General Motors published a report on how many cars it anticipated selling in China this coming year, and how many it would export to other Asian countries from its production in there. Foreign corporations from the celebrated Apple and its supplier, Taiwan's Foxconn, to Canadian and Australian mining corporations have been involved directly in the exploitation of Chinese labor and/or the destruction of the environment, as Buckley documents in his account of mining and dam-building in Tibet. Global corporations and development institutions greet with dismay and panic any effort on the part of the PRC government to slow down development.

Less visibly but even more egregiously, if the PRC has become a "factory of the world," most of us are among the consumers of its products. Consumers around the world enjoy the benefits of its products, oblivious to any connection between what they consume and the outcomes of their consumption at the place of production. Consumers in advanced societies in particular have benefited from the export of exploitation and environmental degradation to the so-called developing societies, of which the PRC is the most prominent. Included among them, ironically, are the laborers whose jobs have been exported to the PRC. At least in the short run, cheap commodities and cheap credit has been their sugar-coated compensation.

With their newfound economic clout, PRC leaders do not hesitate to bully or bribe other states to silence and self-censorship before their abuses of human rights at home and belligerence abroad. Anxiety about jeopardizing business interests has become a refrain in attitudes toward the PRC even on the part of states which pride themselves on their human rights record. There may be good reason in some instances for turning a blind eye to PRC misdeeds, which is by no means uncommon in global politics. What is truly distressing is seemingly willing compliance by governments, international organizations, business corporations, and cultural and educational institutions with the dictatorial demands of a state that openly flaunts its oppressive practices domestically, and displays contempt for international norms and the rights of others, tinged in some cases with sentiments of vengeance for past grievances. Pecuniary gain and long-standing myths about an ancient Chinese civilization are no doubt of primary significance in shaping these responses. But we may ignore at our peril the global forces at work that undermine commitment to popular rights and welfare behind the façade of democracy.

The PRC may have contributed significantly to making authoritarianism respectable, but it did not invent the marriage between capitalism and authoritarian politics, which already in the early 1980s attracted global attention in the economic success of so-called "Neo-Confucian" societies in Eastern Asia. Indeed, one of those societies, Singapore under Prime Minister Lee Kuan Yew, was to serve as a model for the PRC when Deng Xiaoping blessed the turn to capitalism in the early 1990s, following the Tiananmen tragedy of 1989. The downgrading of democracy in favor of economic development has been a central feature of the discourse of "Asian values" that emerged in the 1980s in the cultural self-assertion that accompanied economic success. What the PRC has added is arbitrary lawlessness that caused concern to Lee Kuan Yew himself before his death.

The alliance between economic and political power to the detriment of populations at large is not limited to the PRC, or self-professed anti-democratic authoritarian societies alone, India under Narendra Modi and Turkey under Recep Tayyip Erdogan being prime examples. Democracy is in peril in its original homelands in Europe and North America. We live in times when economic development trumps all other considerations, and the market paradigm rules economic thinking, no matter what the cost in democracy, human rights and social justice. Globalization and the neoliberal economy—two sides of the same coin—have enabled oligarchic concentration of economic wealth and political power, and endowed it with a new prestige. The new oligarchs seek above all to sustain the system of which they are the beneficiaries. One of its architects, Zbigniew Brzezinski, would observe in the mid-1990s on the occasion of a conference on globalization in San Francisco that the urgent issue that faced the new oligarchy was not popular rights but population management in the maintenance of the system—which included "tittytainment" for the eighty percent of the world's population doomed to marginalization under the new regime. PRC leaders' proclivity to uncouth provincialism may raise a few eyebrows here and there, but their proven ability at population management (including "tittytainment") is a cause for envy against the clutter of democracy. Its despotic behavior draws muted murmurs of disapproval, followed by compliance with its wishes. It is little wonder that PRC spokespeople have been emboldened to assert the superiority of their system to disorderly democracies where the struggle for rights has spilled out into the streets!

Whatever the responsibility for the current global crisis of the PRC's economic and political trajectory, if it is to overcome ideological parochialism, criticism needs to recognize that the present crisis is embedded deep in the structures and practices of a developmentalist global capitalism under the neoliberal regime. The PRC is most notable for successful exploitation of the contradictions of this regime, itself having emerged as one of those contradictions. It most saliently displays these contradictions in its very success. Its contributions to the current global crisis are not to be ignored. But responsibility for the end of the world, including the end of the world as we know it, needs to be sought in this more broadly conceived field of contradictions.

****

Those who view "China's rise" with some trepidation if not alarm seem frequently to find their anxiety echoed in a statement attributed to Napoleon Bonaparte: "China is a sleeping giant. Let her sleep, for when she wakes she will move the world." More directly in US cultural and political discourse, which is my main concern here, the idea of "China" and "Chinese" as threats to social well-being and political democracy has a lineage that goes back to conflicts between labor and capital in the late nineteenth century, in which anti-Chinese racism provided the language of labor opposition to immigration from the Qing Dynasty, captured cogently in the title of a book published on the eve of the Chinese Exclusion Act of 1882, *Last Days of the Republic* by Pierton W. Dooner. Interestingly, the Yellow Peril discourse that gained currency after the Boxer Uprising of 1900 was assimilated in Late Qing Dynasty utopias/dystopias, one of which, *The New Era* (*Xin jiyuan*, published 1908), foresaw a rejuvenated China leading the yellow races to conquer Europe and the US in the year 1999. The same theme reappeared in the 1940 film *Drums of Fu Manchu*, where Fu sought to recover Genghis Khan's legacy to lead Asian masses, this time against British imperialism.

In the course of the twentieth century, anxiety about "China's rise" went hand-in-hand with a missionary impulse to save China from itself, as an undercurrent emerging to the surface when the occasion demanded it. Some of us old enough may recollect the statement by US Secretary of State Dean Rusk, in one of his many testimonies before the Senate Foreign Relations Committee in defense of the war in Vietnam, to the effect that if "Red China" was not stopped in Vietnam, "we" might have to fight her in California—which, incidentally, renders questionable the novelty of the idea of "China's rise," though admittedly the rise at the present is a somewhat different "rise" than earlier. Perhaps the most notable recent expression of this anxiety is Samuel Huntington's influential idea (in the PRC as well) of "clash of civilizations," in which "Confucian" states (including the PRC) along with "Islam" represent the most prominent threats to "the West." Popular works of science fiction once again seem to have a flourishing market for works predicting Chinese invasion of US cities.

Given this lineage, there is, then, something risky about the association of "China" with the end of the world, with its origins in the Yellow Peril discourse. The risk is worth the taking, as we face quite different circumstances than those that produced the earlier, Yellow Fever-inflected, notions of the end of the world. The obvious—and the crucial—difference is that it is now possible, and even plausible, to speak with the authority of science that the end of the world is no longer just limited to the end of the world as we know it, but as the end of the world as a literal end-of-history existential possibility. This also places in a different, spatially broader and temporally more extensive perspective the end of history as we know it. And there is no denying the part of the PRC in it, as conceded by the regime and made manifest to the world in the popular uprisings against its misdeeds.

To illustrate this perspective, we may call upon a dystopian science fiction speculation on the end of the world by the distinguished writer Doris Lessing, winner of the Nobel Prize for literature in 2007, in her novel *Shikasta*, which also associates Chinese with the end of the world. Published in 1979, *Shikasta* was the first volume to be published of a five-volume series, entitled *Canopus in Argos Archives*. "Shikasta," a Persian/ Urdu word meaning defeated, broken, and fractured, is the name of a planet that is unmistakably a stand-in for the earth. The novel ranges over the whole history of humanity—its decline and fall—through the eyes of the emissaries of a superior extraterrestrial civilization that had created Shikastan society and guided its evolution. It is in large part a commentary on the twentieth century ("the century of destruction"), with special attention to the 1960s and 1970s. The story is the story of the breakdown of the society the advanced civilization of Canopus had created on the planet Shikasta due to the evil influence of a less benevolent competing civilization that somehow broke through the planet's defenses, destroying the "substance-of-we-feeling" that had held the society together. The result was a society at war with itself. There is something eerily familiar when Lessing writes of this self-destructive society that:

At the top of this structure was the privileged class of technicians and organizers and manipulators, in uniform or out of uniform. An international class of the highly educated in technology, the planners and organizers, were fed, were housed, and interminably travelled, interminably conferred, and formed from country to country a web of experts and administrators whose knowledge of the desperateness of the Shikastan situation caused ideological and national barriers to mean less than nothing among themselves, while in the strata below them these barriers were always intensifying, strengthening. For the crammed and crowding populations were fed slogans and ideologies with the air they breathed, and nowhere was it possible to be free of them.

To make a long story short, this intolerable situation leads to the militarization of society, with armies of youth with no hope in the future organized to fight for survival against mercenary armies recruited to defend the interests of the privileged. The disorder culminates in the replacement of democratic rule by the All-Glorious Pan-European Socialist Democratic Communist Dictatorships for the Preservation of Peace. As the account unfolds, more and more Chinese appear in Europe ("they are everywhere," one of the characters observes). Unable to secure peace on their own, the dictatorships invite the Benevolent Tutelage of the Glorious Chinese Brothers to bring the rebels under control. The youth rebellion which by this time is thoroughly transcontinental, interracial and cosmopolitan continues the struggle against the new Chinese Overlords, befuddling them with mobile resistance and guerilla theater tactics, but above all with the refusal to relinquish individual freedoms that mock the Overlords' assumptions of order, organization and hierarchy. As the Shikasta episode reaches its conclusion, the struggle goes on, with glimmerings of new communities coming into existence from the bottom up. As in other works of dystopian fiction—Evgeny Zamiatin and Ursula LeGuin readily come to mind—the tactics of the youth struggle against oppression and dispossession, and their efforts to rebuild society from the bottom up, resonate with anarchism and practices of everyday popular democracy—as they do also with such struggles in our own day as the Occupy Movements.

Lessing's allegory shares some basic features with the analysis offered in this discussion. At the end of the world in Shikasta humanity survives, but it is the end of civilization, and of the world as the Shikastans have known it. She, too, associates Chinese with the end of the world, but in a different mode than the racially-inflected anti-Chinese fiction. In her account, Chinese are not responsible for the end of the world, which has collapsed under the weight of its contradictions. They are invited to deal with the consequences of the collapse, having survived it themselves for (when Lessing composed her story), they were still not part of that world. Despite their rigidly enforced collective orientation and organizational efficiency, however, they end up confounded themselves for the very same reasons as they are unable to comprehend the values of freedom and individual initiative which are alien to them. The Chinese who appear at the end of the world are not just any Chinese but PR Chinese. *Shikasta* was written during the Cultural Revolution. The characteristics she attributes to the Chinese are those that, then and now, have been associated with Maoist regimentation—at least on the outside, as there was no shortage of dissident if silent PR Chinese even at the height of the Cultural Revolution's totalitarian assault on the individual to create thoroughly socialized subjects.

* * * *

A motivating element in contemporary PRC aspirations to global hegemony, frequently voiced by IR-specialists and policy-makers, is a belief that the current hegemon, the US, is in inexorable decline. It is a belief that is shared by many critics in the US. Issues of ecological catastrophe, deepening economic inequality, attack on social welfare, racism, racial and gender inequality, immigration, cultural identity, religion, gun control, the prison-industrial complex, among others, have created a social situation that strike many as beyond redemption. Social divisions feed uncompromising political divisions that are only barely distinguishable from those of so-called "failed states." US commentators speak freely of corruption in the PRC, but there is little condemnation in mainstream media of corruption in the US, even though it has nearly brought the economy to its knees; at least, PRC leaders are doing something about it, however impure their intentions may seem. Corporate hegemony is almost complete as the corporate economy has gone global both in organization and labor force, and thanks to new technologies, corporations have come to shape everyday culture, and bend education to their interests. At its most fundamental, the corporate economy has come to play a paradigmatic role in reshaping political and educational institutions, which increasingly internalize corporate norms in their functioning. In their dealings with authoritarian regimes from the PRC to Turkey to Saudi Arabia, corporations not only display their indifference to democracy and human rights, or ecological health, but also shore up the legitimacy of authoritarian rule. Transnational corporations eschew their obligations to populations in their nations of origin, parking huge quantities of capital in "offshore" locations to avoid paying the taxes that are crucial to national welfare, but their hold on politics is stronger than ever. With such power imbalances, democracy is in peril. In the pithy observation of a distinguished historian of Chinese religion, John Lagerway, if China has turned into a state-owned corporation, the US appears increasingly as a "corporation-owned state"—what political theorist Sheldon Wolin has dubbed "inverted totalitarianism."

Not the least of the problems faced by US hegemony is endless conflict that the country is mired in. There has been much talk over the last two decades of unipolar US hegemony since the fall of existing socialisms in the early 1990s, and the absorption into capitalism of the PRC. It is indeed the case that at least for part of this period, the US has been able to throw its weight around the globe. But we need to remember also that throughout this period, the US has been at war, its hegemony challenged from a variety of directions, which not incidentally calls into question the meaning of hegemony in relations between nations as well as the relationship of nations to other entities such as ethnicities, indigenous peoples, and religious communities. What is clear at any rate is that endless war, culminating in the so-called "war on terror," has become the new normal, wreaking destruction at home and abroad, wastefully consuming resources that are badly needed to meet popular needs. War also undermines democracy, as wars do, exacerbated at the present by the availability of unprecedented technologies of surveillance and control.

PRC leaders and commentators think that the world is ready for a new hegemony. They may well be right to think so, and they are not alone. They do indeed have every right to boast that they have contributed to human rights significantly by improving the lot of their people. They are by no means oblivious to the ecological and social consequences of development, having become a global leader in green energy production. Endlessly building dams and canals, roads, railroads, and pipelines may be reprehensible, but at least in the short run serve human ends better than endless warfare. For many in the world, especially societies of the Global South, authoritarianism is not much of a concern while aspirations to development a paramount one, and dealing with the institutions of a tightly managed economy likely far more preferable to blackmail by irresponsible and ruthless global banks and hedge funds. Equally important is a sense of shared histories in two centuries or more of economic, political and cultural victimization at the hands of Euro/American imperialism, which is still alive in reconfigured forms.

It is best left to so-called predictioneers to tell whether or not the PRC will fulfill its ambitions to global hegemony. According to some IR scholars both in the US and the PRC, war between the two countries is almost a theoretical certainty. Barring war, predictions concerning the PRC may hardly ignore the possibility also of self-destruction of contemporary society which makes the question of hegemony largely irrelevant. An important question that is often ignored in discourses that assume East/West, or "China/US" binarisms is what others might have to say about such a hegemonic shift. Challengers to the US are not likely to take to Chinese hegemony any more enthusiastically than they do to US hegemony. The world of global modernity, even as it comes to share the single space of global capitalism, is marked by a proliferation of sovereign claims around diverse cultural identities. Then there is the looming ecological crisis against which other scenarios of the future pale to insignificance.

The PRC's candidacy as a global hegemon is also lacking in significant qualifications. The PRC is yet to establish a clear identity that may be projected globally. It remains suspended between wealth and poverty; it may brag developed nation status in terms of overall GDP, but its per capita GDP places it among the poorer nations of the world. If poverty is measured at five dollars a day instead of the self-serving two dollars used by the World Bank and the IMF, nearly 900 million people remain below the poverty level. Ideologically, too, there are serious problems of identity that divide the population. The unity sustained by nationalist aspirations is fragile, while vaguely conceived notions of "glorious tradition" do not sit well with the emergent culture of capitalism. The revolution is dead for all practical purposes, but its legacies continue to haunt the present. A "Confucianized" Marxism that mocks both Confucianism and Marxism may serve short term goals of social control. Its contradictions do not allow plausible claims to identity. The newsletter of one of the PRC's largest private foundations, the Kaifeng Foundation, states in its September 2015 issue that,

> For today's China, it has been proven infeasible either to simply return to traditional values or to simply copy western values. China needs a set of new values that not only combine the merits of both eastern and western thoughts but also accord with the characteristics of the times and the mankind. But so far, we can find not even a trace of such values.

Philosophers, anthropologists and sociologists bear witness to the intense anxieties and anger that pervade popular sentiments. The leadership is quite aware that only continued development may help mask the cultural contradictions that plague the country. If development runs into problems, these contradictions may assume a severity beyond the regime's ability to keep them in check.

Globally, too, the PRC is a "rising power" in search of a paradigm that may provide an identity of its own that may also be appealing to others. While the world may be taken with awe at the PRC's development, there is also widespread dissatisfaction with its expansionist policies, especially among immediate neighbors. There are complaints from African nations whom the PRC has courted assiduously. There is growing resistance in South America to PRC investments for their social and ecological implications. And despite persistent social inequality and political authoritarianism, voices for human rights and democracy are also on the rise globally.

Given its inability so far to address problems of internal authoritarianism (including the suppression of its minorities) and external expansionism, the PRC is ill-equipped to deal with the challenges they present. The lure of its economic largess has failed to dispel suspicion of its motivations and power. Whatever gains it has made in "soft power" through economic largesse and Confucius Institutes is shadowed by not only its expansionist threat to its neighbors but the vigilant pettiness and vindictiveness of its officials—be it enterprising San Francisco consular officials threatening the mayor of Corvallis, Oregon, Xu Lin's vandalism in Portugal, or Foreign Minister Wang Yi's boorish attempt at a press conference in Ottawa in June 2016 to silence a reporter for raising a question about human rights in the PRC. It does not help the PRC's image when its security apparatus resorts to gangsterism not only at home but by kidnapping foreign citizens or supposedly autonomous Hong Kong residents for publishing material the leadership deems offensive. The influential international relations scholar Yan Xuetong bemoans that the PRC has only one true friend: Pakistan. Others have observed that it remains "the loneliest rising power." The "loneliness" is, at least partially, self-inflicted. True, President Xi and his wife recently enjoyed the hospitality of Buckingham Palace in return for promises of closer economic relations to a UK government invariably on the lookout for business interests. Published photos yield the distinct impression that the occasion was not a merry one for either the Queen's family or her guests!

There seems to be a prevalent assumption among policy-makers that the problems of the PRC, and the world, will be resolved if the PRC is more thoroughly integrated into the capitalist world-system. It is a misleading assumption, as the fundamental problems of the world lie not with the PRC but the capitalist world-system itself. In an interview in October 2015, Jack Ma, the head of the internet company Ali Baba, recommended that the US should stop worrying about China and worry about itself. It may be impossible not to worry about the PRC, but the recommendation was a sound one, at least partially, as Ma's own enterprise Ali Baba is part of the problem. The US and the PRC are part of a world system where the most urgent task is to reconsider the developmentalism that has become a "global faith," and explore alternative paths of development where progress is measured not by the GDP figures that drive states, or the profits that drive the corporate economy, but by achievements in long term human welfare and security. Instead of addicting ever more people to their habits of wasteful consumption, so-called advanced societies should be looking for ways to cure their own addictions even as developing societies immunize themselves against its excesses. What is at stake is the world as we know it, our own Shikasta, which is falling apart under the weight of its contradictions. ■

Also available from Prickly Paradigm Press:

Paradigm 1   *Waiting for Foucault, Still*
             Marshall Sahlins

Paradigm 2   *War of the Worlds: What about Peace?*
             Bruno Latour

Paradigm 3   *Against Bosses, Against Oligarchies: A Conversation with
             Richard Rorty*
             Richard Rorty, Derek Nystrom, and Kent Puckett

Paradigm 4   *The Secret Sins of Economics*
             Deirdre McCloskey

Paradigm 5   *New Consensus for Old: Cultural Studies from Left to Right*
             Thomas Frank

Paradigm 6   *Talking Politics: The Substance of Style from Abe to "W"*
             Michael Silverstein

Paradigm 7   *Revolt of the Masscult*
             Chris Lehmann

Paradigm 8   *The Companion Species Manifesto: Dogs, People, and
             Significant Otherness*
             Donna Haraway

Paradigm 9   *9/12: New York After*
             Eliot Weinberger

Paradigm 10 *On the Edges of Anthropology (Interviews)*
             James Clifford

Paradigm 11 *The Thanksgiving Turkey Pardon, the Death of Teddy's Bear,
             and the Sovereign Exception of Guantánamo*
             Magnus Fiskesjö

Paradigm 12 *The Root of Roots: Or, How Afro-American Anthropology
             Got its Start*
             Richard Price and Sally Price

Paradigm 13 *What Happened to Art Criticism?*
             James Elkins

Paradigm 14 *Fragments of an Anarchist Anthropology*
             David Graeber

Paradigm 15 *Enemies of Promise: Publishing, Perishing, and the Eclipse
             of Scholarship*
             Lindsay Waters

Paradigm 16 *The Empire's New Clothes: Paradigm Lost, and Regained*
             Harry Harootunian

continued

Paradigm 17 *Intellectual Complicity: The State and Its Destructions*
Bruce Kapferer

Paradigm 18 *The Hitman's Dilemma: Or, Business, Personal and Impersonal*
Keith Hart

Paradigm 19 *The Law in Shambles*
Thomas Geoghegan

Paradigm 20 *The Stock Ticker and the Superjumbo: How The Democrats Can Once Again Become America's Dominant Political Party*
Rick Perlstein

Paradigm 21 *Museum, Inc.: Inside the Global Art World*
Paul Werner

Paradigm 22 *Neo-Liberal Genetics: The Myths and Moral Tales of Evolutionary Psychology*
Susan McKinnon

Paradigm 23 *Phantom Calls: Race and the Globalization of the NBA*
Grant Farred

Paradigm 24 *The Turn of the Native*
Eduardo Viveiros de Castro, Flávio Gordon, and Francisco Araújo

Paradigm 25 *The American Game: Capitalism, Decolonization, World Domination, and Baseball*
John D. Kelly

Paradigm 26 *"Culture" and Culture: Traditional Knowledge and Intellectual Rights*
Manuela Carneiro da Cunha

Paradigm 27 *Reading* Legitimation Crisis *in Tehran: Iran and the Future of Liberalism*
Danny Postel

Paradigm 28 *Anti-Semitism and Islamophobia: Hatreds Old and New in Europe*
Matti Bunzl

Paradigm 29 *Neomedievalism, Neoconservatism, and the War on Terror*
Bruce Holsinger

Paradigm 30 *Understanding Media: A Popular Philosophy*
Dominic Boyer

Paradigm 31 *Pasta and Pizza*
Franco La Cecla

Paradigm 32 *The Western Illusion of Human Nature: With Reflections on the Long History of Hierarchy, Equality, and the Sublimation of Anarchy in the West, and Comparative Notes on Other Conceptions of the Human Condition*
Marshall Sahlins

Paradigm 33 *Time and Human Language Now*
Jonathan Boyarin and Martin Land

Paradigm 34 *American Counterinsurgency: Human Science and the Human Terrain*
Roberto J. González

Paradigm 35 *The Counter-Counterinsurgency Manual: Or, Notes on Demilitarizing American Society*
Network of Concerned Anthropologists

Paradigm 36 *Are the Humanities Inconsequent? Interpreting Marx's Riddle of the Dog*
Jerome McGann

Paradigm 37 *The Science of Passionate Interests: An Introduction to Gabriel Tarde's Economic Anthropology*
Bruno Latour and Vincent Antonin Lépinay

Paradigm 38 *Pacification and its Discontents*
Kurt Jacobsen

Paradigm 39 *An Anthropological Theory of the Corporation*
Ira Bashkow

Paradigm 40 *The Great Debate About Art*
Roy Harris

Paradigm 41 *The Inconstancy of the Indian Soul: The Encounter of Catholics and Cannibals in 16th-Century Brazil*
Eduardo Viveiros de Castro

Paradigm 42 *The Ecology of Others: Anthropology and the Question of Nature*
Philippe Descola

Paradigm 43 *Pastoral in Palestine*
Neil Hertz

Paradigm 44 *The Culture of Ethics*
Franco La Cecla and Piero Zanini

Paradigm 45 *2001 and Counting: Kubrick, Nietzsche, and Anthropology*
Bruce Kapferer

Paradigm 46 *Data: Now Bigger and Better!*
Edited by Tom Boellstorff and Bill Maurer

continued

Paradigm 47 *Jean-Pierre Vernant: From the Maquis to the Polis*
Jean-Pierre Vernant, edited and with preface
by François Hartog

Paradigm 48 *Confucius Institutes: Academic Malware*
Marshall Sahlins

Paradigm 49 *The Science of Myths and Vice Versa*
Gregory Schrempp

Paradigm 50 *Community of Scholars, Community of Teachers*
Judith Shapiro

Paradigm 51 *"Man—with Variations": Interviews with Franz Boas
and Colleagues, 1937*
Joseph Mitchell, edited and with an introduction
by Robert Brightman

Paradigm 52 *Making Trouble: Surrealism and the Human Sciences*
Derek Sayer

Paradigm 53 *Complicities: The People's Republic of China
in Global Capitalism*
Arif Dirlik